POEMS

Vol. I.

POEMS

Vol. I

POEMS

BY GEORGE MEREDITH

VOLUME I

LONDON
CONSTABLE & COMPANY Ltd
1909

CONTENTS

THE PROMISE IN DISTURBANCE

How low when angels fall their black descent,
Our primal thunder tells: known is the pain
Of music, that nigh throning wisdom went,
And one false note cast wailful to the insane.
Now seems the language heard of Love as rain
To make a mire where fruitfulness was meant.
The golden harp gives out a jangled strain,
Too like revolt from heaven's Omnipotent.
But listen in the thought; so may there come
Conception of a newly-added chord,
Commanding space beyond where ear has home.
In labour of the trouble at its fount,
Leads Life to an intelligible Lord
The rebel discords up the sacred mount.

MODERN LOVE

I

By this he knew sne wept with waking eyes:
That, at his hand's light quiver by her head,
The strange low sobs that shook their common bed,
Were called into her with a sharp surprise,
And strangled mute, like little gaping snakes,
Dreadfully venomous to him.   She lay
Stone-still, and the long darkness flowed away
With muffled pulses.   Then, as midnight makes
Her giant heart of Memory and Tears
Drink the pale drug of silence, and so beat
Sleep's heavy measure, they from head to feet
Were moveless, looking through their dead black years,
By vain regret scrawled over the blank wall.
Like sculptured effigies they might be seen
Upon their marriage-tomb, the sword between;
Each wishing for the sword that severs all.

II

It ended, and the morrow brought the task.
Her eyes were guilty gates, that let him in
By shutting all too zealous for their sin :
Each sucked a secret, and each wore a mask.
But, oh, the bitter taste her beauty had !
He sickened as at breath of poison-flowers :
A languid humour stole among the hours,
And if their smiles encountered, he went mad,
And raged deep inward, till the light was brown
Before his vision, and the world forgot,
Looked wicked as some old dull murder-spot.
A star with lurid beams, she seemed to crown
The pit of infamy : and then again
He fainted on his vengefulness, and strove
To ape the magnanimity of love,
And smote himself, a shuddering heap of pain.

III

This was the woman; what now of the man?
But pass him.   If he comes beneath a heel,
He shall be crushed until he cannot feel,
Or, being callous, haply till he can.
But he is nothing: — nothing?   Only mark
The rich light striking out from her on him!
Ha! what a sense it is when her eyes swim
Across the man she singles, leaving dark
All else!   Lord God, who mad'st the thing so fair,
See that I am drawn to her even now!
It cannot be such harm on her cool brow
To put a kiss?   Yet if I meet him there!
But she is mine!   Ah, no! I know too well
I claim a star whose light is overcast:
I claim a phantom-woman in the Past.
The hour has struck, though I heard not the bell!

IV

All other joy of life he strove to warm,
And magnify, and catch them to his lip:
But they had suffered shipwreck with the ship,
And gazed upon him sallow from the storm.
Or if Delusion came, 't was but to show
The coming minute mock the one that went.
Cold as a mountain in its star-pitched tent,
Stood high Philosophy, less friend than foe:
Whom self-caged Passion, from its prison-bars,
Is always watching with a wondering hate.
Not till the fire is dying in the grate,
Look we for any kinship with the stars.
Oh, wisdom never comes when it is gold,
And the great price we pay for it full worth:
We have it only when we are half earth.
Little avails that coinage to the old!

V

A message from her set his brain aflame.
A world of household matters filled her mind,
Wherein he saw hypocrisy designed:
She treated him as something that is tame,
And but at other provocation bites.
Familiar was her shoulder in the glass,
Through that dark rain: yet it may come to pass
That a changed eye finds such familiar sights
More keenly tempting than new loveliness.
The ' What has been ' a moment seemed his own:
The splendours, mysteries, dearer because known,
Nor less divine: Love's inmost sacredness,
Called to him, ' Come ! '— In his restraining start,
Eyes nurtured to be looked at, scarce could see
A wave of the great waves of Destiny
Convulsed at a checked impulse of the heart.

VI

It chanced his lips did meet her forehead cool.
She had no blush, but slanted down her eye.
Shamed nature, then, confesses love can die:
And most she punishes the tender fool
Who will believe what honours her the most!
Dead! is it dead? She has a pulse, and flow
Of tears, the price of blood-drops, as I know,
For whom the midnight sobs around Love's ghost,
Since then I heard her, and so will sob on.
The love is here; it has but changed its aim.
O bitter barren woman! what's the name?
The name, the name, the new name thou hast won?
Behold me striking the world's coward stroke!
That will I not do, though the sting is dire.
— Beneath the surface this, while by the fire
They sat, she laughing at a quiet joke.

VII

She issues radiant from her dressing-room,
Like one prepared to scale an upper sphere:
— By stirring up a lower, much I fear!
How deftly that oiled barber lays his bloom!
That long-shanked dapper Cupid with frisked curls,
Can make known women torturingly fair;
The gold-eyed serpent dwelling in rich hair,
Awakes beneath his magic whisks and twirls.
His art can take the eyes from out my head,
Until I see with eyes of other men;
While deeper knowledge crouches in its den,
And sends a spark up: — is it true we are wed?
Yea! filthiness of body is most vile,
But faithlessness of heart I do hold worse.
The former, it were not so great a curse
To read on the steel-mirror of her smile.

VIII

Yet it was plain she struggled, and that salt
Of righteous feeling made her pitiful.
Poor twisting worm, so queenly beautiful!
Where came the cleft between us? whose the fault?
My tears are on thee, that have rarely dropped
As balm for any bitter wound of mine:
My breast will open for thee at a sign!
But, no: we are two reed-pipes, coarsely stopped:
The God once filled them with his mellow breath;
And they were music till he flung them down,
Used! used!   Hear now the discord-loving clown
Puff his gross spirit in them, worse than death!
I do not know myself without thee more:
In this unholy battle I grow base:
If the same soul be under the same face,
Speak, and a taste of that old time restore!

IX

He felt the wild beast in him betweenwhiles
So masterfully rude, that he would grieve
To see the helpless delicate thing receive
His guardianship through certain dark defiles.
Had he not teeth to rend, and hunger too?
But still he spared her.   Once: 'Have you no fear?'
He said: 't was dusk; she in his grasp; none near.
She laughed: 'No, surely; am I not with you?'
And uttering that soft starry 'you,' she leaned
Her gentle body near him, looking up;
And from her eyes, as from a poison-cup,
He drank until the flittering eyelids screened.
Devilish malignant witch! and oh, young beam
Of heaven's circle-glory!   Here thy shape
To squeeze like an intoxicating grape —
I might, and yet thou goest safe, supreme.

8.

But where began the change; and what's my crime?
The wretch condemned, who has not been arraigned,
Chafes at his sentence.   Shall I, unsustained,
Drag on Love's nerveless body thro' all time?
I must have slept, since now I wake.   Prepare,
You lovers, to know Love a thing of moods:
Not like hard life, of laws.   In Love's deep woods,
I dreamt of loyal Life: — the offence is there!
Love's jealous woods about the sun are curled;
At least, the sun far brighter there did beam.—
My crime is, that the puppet of a dream,
I plotted to be worthy of the world.
Oh, had I with my darling helped to mince
The facts of life, you still had seen me go
With hindward feather and with forward toe,
Her much-adored delightful Fairy Prince!

XI

Out in the yellow meadows, where the bee
Hums by us with the honey of the Spring,
And showers of sweet notes from the larks on wing,
Are dropping like a noon-dew, wander we.
Or is it now? or was it then? for now,
As then, the larks from running rings pour showers
The golden foot of May is on the flowers,
And friendly shadows dance upon her brow.
What's this, when Nature swears there is no change
To challenge eyesight?   Now, as then, the grace
Of heaven seems holding earth in its embrace.
Nor eyes, nor heart, has she to feel it strange?
Look, woman, in the West.   There wilt thou see
An amber cradle near the sun's decline :
Within it, featured even in death divine,
Is lying a dead infant, slain by thee.

XII

Not solely that the Future she destroys,
And the fair life which in the distance lies
For all men, beckoning out from dim rich skies:
Nor that the passing hour's supporting joys
Have lost the keen-edged flavour, which begat
Distinction in old times, and still should breed
Sweet Memory, and Hope, — earth's modest seed,
And heaven's high-prompting: not that the world is flat
Since that soft-luring creature I embraced,
Among the children of Illusion went:
Methinks with all this loss I were content,
If the mad Past, on which my foot is based,
Were firm, or might be blotted: but the whole
Of life is mixed: the mocking Past will stay:
And if I drink oblivion of a day,
So shorten I the stature of my soul.

XIII

'I play for Seasons ; not Eternities !'
Says Nature, laughing on her way.   'So must
All those whose stake is nothing more than dust !'
And lo, she wins, and of her harmonies
She is full sure !   Upon her dying rose,
She drops a look of fondness, and goes by,
Scarce any retrospection in her eye ;
For she the laws of growth most deeply knows,
Whose hands bear, here, a seed-bag — there, an urn.
Pledged she herself to aught, 't would mark her end !
This lesson of our only visible friend,
Can we not teach our foolish hearts to learn ?
Yes! yes ! — but, oh, our human rose is fair
Surpassingly !   Lose calmly Love's great bliss,
When the renewed for ever of a kiss
Whirls life within the shower of loosened hair !

XIV

What soul would bargain for a cure that brings
Contempt the nobler agony to kill?
Rather let me bear on the bitter ill,
And strike this rusty bosom with new stings!
It seems there is another veering fit,
Since on a gold-haired lady's eyeballs pure,
I looked with little prospect of a cure,
The while her mouth's red bow loosed shafts of wit.
Just heaven! can it be true that jealousy
Has decked the woman thus? and does her head
Swim somewhat for possessions forfeited?
Madam, you teach me many things that be.
I open an old book, and there I find,
That 'Women still may love whom they deceive.'
Such love I prize not, madam: by your leave,
The game you play at is not to my mind.

XV

I think she sleeps: it must be sleep, when low
Hangs that abandoned arm toward the floor;
The face turned with it.   Now make fast the door.
Sleep on: it is your husband, not your foe.
The Poet's black stage-lion of wronged love,
Frights not our modern dames:— well if he did!
Now will I pour new light upon that lid,
Full-sloping like the breasts beneath.   'Sweet dove,
Your sleep is pure.   Nay, pardon: I disturb.
I do not? good!'   Her waking infant-stare
Grows woman to the burden my hands bear:
Her own handwriting to me when no curb
Was left on Passion's tongue.   She trembles through;
A woman's tremble — the whole instrument:—
I show another letter lately sent.
The words are very like: the name is new.

XVI

In our old shipwrecked days there was an hour,
When in the firelight steadily aglow,
Joined slackly, we beheld the red chasm grow
Among the clicking coals.   Our library-bower
That eve was left to us: and hushed we sat
As lovers to whom Time is whispering.
From sudden-opened doors we heard them sing:
The nodding elders mixed good wine with chat.
Well knew we that Life's greatest treasure lay
With us, and of it was our talk.   'Ah, yes!
Love dies!' I said: I never thought it less.
She yearned to me that sentence to unsay.
Then when the fire domed blackening, I found
Her cheek was salt against my kiss, and swift
Up the sharp scale of sobs her breast did lift: —
Now am I haunted by that taste! that sound!

XVII

At dinner, she is hostess, I am host.
Went the feast ever cheerfuller? She keeps
The Topic over intellectual deeps
In buoyancy afloat.   They see no ghost.
With sparkling surface-eyes we ply the ball:
It is in truth a most contagious game:
HIDING THE SKELETON, shall be its name.
Such play as this, the devils might appal!
But here's the greater wonder; in that we
Enamoured of an acting nought can tire,
Each other, like true hypocrites, admire;
Warm-lighted looks, Love's ephemerioe,
Shoot gaily o'er the dishes and the wine.
We waken envy of our happy lot.
Fast, sweet, and golden, shows the marriage-knot.
Dear guests, you now have seen Love's corpse-light shine.

XVIII

Here Jack and Tom are paired with Moll and Meg.
Curved open to the river-reach is seen
A country merry-making on the green.
Fair space for signal shakings of the leg.
That little screwy fiddler from his booth,
Whence flows one nut-brown stream, commands the joints
Of all who caper here at various points.
I have known rustic revels in my youth :
The May-fly pleasures of a mind at ease.
An early goddess was a county lass :
A charmed Amphion-oak she tripped the grass.
What life was that I lived ? The life of these ?
Heaven keep them happy ! Nature they seem near
They must, I think, be wiser than I am ;
They have the secret of the bull and lamb.
'T is true that when we trace its source, 't is beer.

XIX

No state is enviable.   To the luck alone
Of some few favoured men I would put claim.
I bleed, but her who wounds I will not blame.
Have I not felt her heart as 't were my own
Beat thro' me ? could I hurt her ? heaven and hell !
But I could hurt her cruelly !   Can I let
My Love's old time-piece to another set,
Swear it can't stop, and must for ever swell ? !
Sure, that's one way Love drifts into the mart
Where goat-legged buyers throng.   I see not plain : —
My meaning is, it must not be again.
Great God ! the maddest gambler throws his heart.
If any state be enviable on earth,
'T is yon born idiot's, who, as days go by,
Still rubs his hands before him, like a fly.
In a queer sort of meditative mirth.

XX

I am not of those miserable males
Who sniff at vice, and, daring not to snap,
Do therefore hope for heaven. I take the hap
Of all my deeds. The wind that fills my sails,
Propels; but I am helmsman. Am I wrecked,
I know the devil has sufficient weight
To bear: I lay it not on him, or fate.
Besides, he's damned. That man I do suspect
A coward, who would burden the poor deuce
With what ensues from his own slipperiness.
I have just found a wanton-scented tress
In an old desk, dusty for lack of use.
Of days and nights it is demonstrative,
That, like some aged star, gleam luridly.
If for those times I must ask charity,
Have I not any charity to give?

XXI

We three are on the cedar-shadowed lawn;
My friend being third.   He who at love once laughed,
Is in the weak rib by a fatal shaft
Struck through, and tells his passion's bashful dawn
And radiant culmination, glorious crown,
When 'this' she said: went 'thus': most wondrous she,
Our eyes grow white, encountering: that we are three,
Forgetful; then together we look down.
But he demands our blessing; is convinced
That words of wedded lovers must bring good.
We question; if we dare! or if we should!
And pat him, with light laugh.   We have not winced.
Next, she has fallen.   Fainting points the sign
To happy things in wedlock.   When she wakes,
She looks the star that thro' the cedar shakes:
Her lost moist hand clings mortally to mine.

XXII

What may the woman labour to confess?
There is about her mouth a nervous twitch.
'T is something to be told, or hidden :— which?
I get a glimpse of hell in this mild guess.
She has desires of touch, as if to feel
That all the household things are things she knew.
She stops before the glass.   What sight in view?
A face that seems the latest to reveal!
For she turns from it hastily, and tossed
Irresolute, steals shadow-like to where
I stand; and wavering pale before me there,
Her tears fall still as oak-leaves after frost.
She will not speak.   I will not ask.   We are
League-sundered by the silent gulf between.
You burly lovers on the village green,
Yours is a lower, and a happier star!

XXIII

'T is Christmas weather, and a country house
Receives us: rooms are full: we can but get
An attic-crib.   Such lovers will not fret
At that, it is half-said.   The great carouse
Knocks hard upon the midnight's hollow door,
But when I knock at hers, I see the pit.
Why did I come here in that dullard fit?
I enter, and lie couched upon the floor.
Passing, I caught the coverlet's quick beat: —
Come, Shame, burn to my soul! and Pride, and Pain—
Foul demons that have tortured me, enchain!
Out in the freezing darkness the lambs bleat.
The small bird stiffens in the low starlight.
I know not how, but shuddering as I slept,
I dreamed a banished angel to me crept:
My feet were nourished on her breasts all night.

XXIV

The misery is greater, as I live!
To know her flesh so pure, so keen **her sense,**
That she does penance now for no offence,
Save against Love.   The less can I forgive!
The less can I forgive, though I adore
That cruel lovely pallor which surrounds
Her footsteps; and the low vibrating sounds
That come on me, as from a magic shore.
Low are they, but most subtle to find out
The shrinking soul.   Madam, 't is understood
When women play upon their womanhood;
It means, a Season gone.   And yet I doubt
But I am duped.   That nun-like look waylays
My fancy.   Oh! I do but wait a sign!
Pluck out the eyes of pride! thy mouth to mine!
Never! though I die thirsting.   Go thy ways!

XXV

You like not that French novel? Tell me why.
You think it quite unnatural. Let us see.
The actors are, it seems, the usual three:
Husband, and wife, and lover. She — but fie!
In England we'll not hear of it. Edmond,
The lover, her devout chagrin doth share;
Blanc-mange and absinthe are his penitent fare,
Till his pale aspect makes her over-fond:
So, to preclude fresh sin, he tries rosbif.
Meantime the husband is no more abused:
Auguste forgives her ere the tear is used.
Then hangeth all on one tremendous IF: —
If she will choose between them. She does choose;
And takes her husband, like a proper wife.
Unnatural? My dear, these things are life:
And life, some think, is worthy of the Muse.

XXVI

Love ere he bleeds, an eagle in high skies,
Has earth beneath his wings : from reddened eve
He views the rosy dawn.   In vain they weave
The fatal web below while far he flies.
But when the arrow strikes him, there 's a change.
He moves but in the track of his spent pain,
Whose red drops are the links of a harsh chain,
Binding him to the ground, with narrow range.
A subtle serpent then has Love become.
I had the eagle in my bosom erst :
Henceforward with the serpent I am cursed.
I can interpret where the mouth is dumb.
Speak, and I see the side-lie of a truth.
Perchance my heart may pardon you this deed :
But be no coward : — you that made Love bleed,
You must bear all the venom of his tooth !

XXVII

Distraction is the panacea, Sir!
I hear my oracle of Medicine say.
Doctor! that same specific yesterday
I tried, and the result will not deter
A second trial.   Is the devil's line
Of golden hair, or raven black, composed?
And does a cheek, like any sea-shell rosed,
Or clear as widowed sky, seem most divine?
No matter, so I taste forgetfulness.
And if the devil snare me, body and mind,
Here gratefully I score : — he seemëd kind,
When not a soul would comfort my distress!
O sweet new world, in which I rise new made!
O Lady, once I gave love : now I take!
Lady, I must be flattered.   Shouldst thou wake
The passion of a demon, be not afraid.

XXVIII

I must be flattered.   The imperious
Desire speaks out.   Lady, I am content
To play with you the game of Sentiment,
And with you enter on paths perilous;
But if across your beauty I throw light,
To make it threefold, it must be all mine.
First secret; then avowed.   For I must shine
Envied, — I, lessened in my proper sight!
Be watchful of your beauty, Lady dear!
How much hangs on that lamp you cannot tell.
Most earnestly I pray you, tend it well:
And men shall see me as a burning sphere;
And men shall mark you eyeing me, and groan
To be the God of such a grand sunflower!
I feel the promptings of Satanic power,
While you do homage unto me alone.

XXIX

Am I failing ?   For no longer can I cast
A glory round about this head of gold.
Glory she wears, but springing from the mould ;
Not like the consecration of the Past !
Is my soul beggared ?   Something more than earth
I cry for still : I cannot be at peace
In having Love upon a mortal lease.
I cannot take the woman at her worth !
Where is the ancient wealth wherewith I clothed
Our human nakedness, and could endow
With spiritual splendour a white brow
That else had grinned at me the fact I loathed ?
A kiss is but a kiss now ! and no wave
Of a great flood that whirls me to the sea.
But, as you will ! we 'll sit contentedly,
And eat our pot of honey on the grave.

XXX

What are we first ?   First, animals ; and next
Intelligences at a leap ; on whom
Pale lies the distant shadow of the tomb,
And all that draweth on the tomb for text.
Into which state comes Love, the crowning sun :
Beneath whose light the shadow loses form.
We are the lords of life, and life is warm.
Intelligence and instinct now are one.
But nature says : ' My children most they seem
When they least know me : therefore I decree
That they shall suffer.'   Swift doth young Love flee,
And we stand wakened, shivering from our dream.
Then if we study Nature we are wise.
Thus do the few who live but with the day :
The scientific animals are they. —
Lady, this is my sonnet to your eyes.

XXXI

This golden head has wit in it. I live
Again, and a far higher life, near her.
Some women like a young philosopher;
Perchance because he is diminutive.
For woman's manly god must not exceed
Proportions of the natural nursing size.
Great poets and great sages draw no prize
With women : but the little lap-dog breed,
Who can be hugged, or on a mantel-piece
Perched up for adoration, these obtain
Her homage.   And of this we men are vain?
Of this! 'T is ordered for the world's increase!
Small flattery! Yet she has that rare gift
To beauty, Common Sense. I am approved.
It is not half so nice as being loved,
And yet I do prefer it.   What's my drift?

XXXII

Full faith I have she holds that rarest gift
To beauty, Common Sense. To see her lie
With her fair visage an inverted sky
Bloom-covered, while the underlids uplift,
Would almost wreck the faith; but when her mouth
(Can it kiss sweetly? sweetly!) would address
The inner me that thirsts for her no less,
And has so long been languishing in drouth,
I feel that I am matched; that I am man!
One restless corner of my heart or head,
That holds a dying something never dead,
Still frets, though Nature giveth all she can.
It means, that woman is not, I opine,
Her sex's antidote. Who seeks the asp
For serpent's bites? 'T would calm me could I clasp
Shrieking Bacchantes with their souls of wine!

XXXIII

'In Paris, at the Louvre, there have I seen
The sumptuously-feathered angel pierce
Prone Lucifer, descending. Looked he fierce,
Showing the fight a fair one? Too serene!
The young Pharsalians did not disarray
Less willingly their locks of floating silk:
That suckling mouth of his, upon the milk
Of heaven might still be feasting through the fray.
Oh, Raphael! when men the Fiend do fight,
They conquer not upon such easy terms.
Half serpent in the struggle grow these worms.
And does he grow half human, all is right.'
This to my Lady in a distant spot,
Upon the theme: *While mind is mastering clay,
Gross clay invades it.* If the spy you play,
My wife, read this! Strange love talk, is it not?

XXXIV

Madam would speak with me.   So, now it comes:
The Deluge or else Fire !   She 's well ; she thanks
My husbandship.   Our chain on silence clanks.
Time leers between, above his twiddling thumbs.
Am I quite well ?   Most excellent in health !
The journals, too, I diligently peruse.
Vesuvius is expected to give news :
Niagara is no noisier.   By stealth
Our eyes dart scrutinizing snakes.   She 's glad
I 'm happy, says her quivering under-lip.
' And are not you ? '   ' How can I be ? '   ' Take ship !
For happiness is somewhere to be had.'
' Nowhere for me ! '   Her voice is barely heard.
I am not melted, and make no pretence.
With commonplace I freeze her, tongue and sense.
Niagara or Vesuvius is deferred.

XXXV

It is no vulgar nature I have wived.
Secretive, sensitive, she takes a wound
Deep to her soul, as if the sense had swooned,
And not a thought of vengeance had survived.
No confidences has she: but relief
Must come to one whose suffering is acute.
O have a care of natures that are mute!
They punish you in acts: their steps are brief.
What is she doing? What does she demand
From Providence or me? She is not one
Long to endure this torpidly, and shun
The drugs that crowd about a woman's hand.
At Forfeits during snow we played, and I
Must kiss her. 'Well performed!' I said: then she:
''T is hardly worth the money, you agree?'
Save her? What for? To act this wedded lie!

XXXVI

My Lady unto Madam makes her bow.
The charm of women is, that even while
You 're probed by them for tears, you yet may smile,
Nay, laugh outright, as I have done just now.
The interview was gracious: they anoint
(To me aside) each other with fine praise:
Discriminating compliments they raise,
That hit with wondrous aim on the weak point:
My Lady's nose of Nature might complain.
It is not fashioned aptly to express
Her character of large-browed steadfastness.
But Madam says: Thereof she may be vain!
Now, Madam's faulty feature is a glazed
And inaccessible eye, that has soft fires,
Wide gates, at love-time only. This admirer
My Lady. At the two I stand amazed.

XXXVII

Along the garden terrace, under which
A purple valley (lighted at its edge
By smoky torch-flame on the long cloud-ledge
Whereunder dropped the chariot), glimmers rich,
A quiet company we pace, and wait
The dinner-bell in prae-digestive calm.
So sweet up violet banks the Southern balm
Breathes round, we care not if the bell be late:
Though here and there grey seniors question Time
In irritable coughings.   With slow foot
The low rosed moon, the face of Music mute,
Begins among her silent bars to climb.
As in and out, in silvery dusk, we thread,
I hear the laugh of Madam, and discern
My Lady's heel before me at each turn.
Our tragedy, is it alive or dead?

XXXVIII

Give to imagination some pure light
In human form to fix it, or you shame
The devils with that hideous human game: —
Imagination urging appetite!
Thus fallen have earth's greatest Gogmagogs,
Who dazzle us, whom we can not revere:
Imagination is the charioteer
That, in default of better, drives the hogs.
So, therefore, my dear Lady, let me love!
My soul is arrowy to the light in you.
You know me that I never can renew
The bond that woman broke: what would you have?
'T is Love, or Vileness! not a choice between,
Save petrifaction! What does Pity here?
She killed a thing, and now it's dead, 't is dear.
Oh, when you counsel me, think what you mean!

XXXIX

She yields : my Lady in her noblest mood
Has yielded : she, my golden-crownëd rose !
The bride of every sense ! more sweet than those
Who breathe the violet breath of maidenhood.
O visage of still music in the sky !
Soft moon !   I feel thy song, my fairest friend !
True harmony within can apprehend
Dumb harmony without.   And hark ! 't is nigh !
Belief has struck the note of sound : a gleam
Of living silver shows me where she shook
Her long white fingers down the shadowy brook,
That sings her song, half waking, half in dream.
What two come here to mar this heavenly tune ?
A man is one : the woman bears my name,
And honour.   Their hands touch !   Am I still tame ?
God, what a dancing spectre seems the moon !

XL

I bade my Lady think what she might mean.
Know I my meaning, I ?   Can I love one,
And yet be jealous of another ?   None
Commits such folly.   Terrible Love, I ween,
Has might, even dead, half sighing to upheave
The lightless seas of selfishness amain:
Seas that in a man's heart have no rain
To fall and still them.   Peace can I achieve,
By turning to this fountain-source of woe,
This woman, who's to Love as fire to wood ?
She breathed the violet breath of maidenhood
Against my kisses once ! but I say, No !
The thing is mocked at !   Helplessly afloat,
I know not what I do, whereto I strive,
The dread that my old love may be alive,
Has seized my nursling new love by the throat.

XLI

How many a thing which we cast to the ground,
When others pick it up becomes a gem!
We grasp at all the wealth it is to them;
And by reflected light its worth is found.
Yet for us still 't is nothing! and that zeal
Of false appreciation quickly fades.
This truth is little known to human shades,
How rare from their own instinct 't is to feel!
They waste the soul with spurious desire,
That is not the ripe flame upon the bough.
We two have taken up a lifeless vow
To rob a living passion: dust for fire!
Madam is grave, and eyes the clock that tells
Approaching midnight. We have struck despair
Into two hearts. O, look we like a pair
Who for fresh nuptials joyfully yield all else?

XLII

I am to follow her.   There is much grace
In woman when thus bent on martyrdom.
They think that dignity of soul may come,
Perchance, with dignity of body.   Base!
But I was taken by that air of cold
And statuesque sedateness, when she said
'I'm going'; lit a taper, bowed her head,
And went, as with the stride of Pallas bold.
Fleshly indifference horrible!   The hands
Of Time now signal: O, she's safe from me!
Within those secret walls what do I see?
Where first she set the taper down she stands:
Not Pallas: Hebe shamed!   Thoughts black as death,
Like a stirred pool in sunshine break.   Her wrists
I catch: she faltering, as she half resists,
'You love ... ? love ... ? love ... ? ' all on an indrawn
    breath.

XLIII

Mark where the pressing wind shoots javelin-like,
Its skeleton shadow on the broad-backed wave!
Here is a fitting spot to dig Love's grave;
Here where the ponderous breakers plunge and strike,
And dart their hissing tongues high up the sand:
In hearing of the ocean, and in sight
Of those ribbed wind-streaks running into white.
If I the death of Love had deeply planned,
I never could have made it half so sure,
As by the unblest kisses which upbraid
The full-waked sense; or failing that, degrade!
'T is morning: but no morning can restore
What we have forfeited.   I see no sin:
The wrong is mixed.   In tragic life, God wot,
No villain need be!   Passions spin the plot:
We are betrayed by what is false within.

XLIV

They say, that Pity in Love's service dwells,
A porter at the rosy temple's gate.
I missed him going : but it is my fate
To come upon him now beside his wells ;
Whereby I know that I Love's temple leave,
And that the purple doors have closed behind.
Poor soul ! if in those early days unkind,
Thy power to sting had been but power to grieve
We now might with an equal spirit meet,
And not be matched like innocence and vice.
She for the Temple's worship has paid price,
And takes the coin of Pity as a cheat.
She sees through simulation to the bone :
What 's best in her impels her to the worst :
Never, she cries, shall Pity soothe Love's thirst,
Or foul hypocrisy for truth atone !

XLV

It is the season of the sweet wild rose,
My Lady's emblem in the heart of me!
So golden-crownëd shines she gloriously,
And with that softest dream of blood she glows:
Mild as an evening heaven round Hesper bright!
I pluck the flower, and smell it, and revive
The time when in her eyes I stood alive.
I seem to look upon it out of Night.
Here 's Madam, stepping hastily.   Her whims
Bid her demand the flower, which I let drop.
As I proceed, I feel her sharply stop,
And crush it under heel with trembling limbs.
She joins me in a cat-like way, and talks
Of company, and even condescends
To utter laughing scandal of old friends.
These are the summer days, and these our walks.

XLVI

At last we parley: we so strangely dumb
In such a close communion ! It befell
About the sounding of the Matin-bell,
And lo ! her place was vacant, and the hum
Of loneliness was round me. Then I rose,
And my disordered brain did guide my foot
To that old wood where our first love-salute
Was interchanged: the source of many throes !
There did I see her, not alone. I moved
Toward her, and made proffer of my arm.
She took it simply, with no rude alarm ;
And that disturbing shadow passed reproved.
I felt the pained speech coming, and declared
My firm belief in her, ere she could speak.
A ghastly morning came into her cheek,
While with a widening soul on me she stared.

XLVII

We saw the swallows gathering in the sky,
And in the osier-isle we heard them noise.
We had not to look back on summer joys,
Or forward to a summer of bright dye:
But in the largeness of the evening earth
Our spirits grew as we went side by side.
The hour became her husband and my bride.
Love that had robbed us so, thus blessed our dearth!
The pilgrims of the year waxed very loud
In multitudinous chatterings, as the flood
Full brown came from the West, and like pale blood
Expanded to the upper crimson cloud.
Love that had robbed us of immortal things,
This little moment mercifully gave,
Where I have seen across the twilight wave
The swan sail with her young beneath her wings.

XLVIII

Their sense is with their senses all mixed in,
Destroyed by subtleties these women are!
More brain, O Lord, more brain! or we shall mar
Utterly this fair garden we might win.
Behold! I looked for peace, and thought it near.
Our inmost hearts had opened, each to each.
We drank the pure daylight of honest speech.
Alas! that was the fatal draught, I fear.
For when of my lost Lady came the word,
This woman, O this agony of flesh!
Jealous devotion bade her break the mesh,
That I might seek that other like a bird.
I do adore the nobleness! despise
The act!   She has gone forth, I know not where.
Will the hard world my sentience of her share?
I feel the truth; so let the world surmise.

XLIX

He found her by the ocean's moaning verge,
Nor any wicked change in her discerned;
And she believed his old love had returned,
Which was her exultation, and her scourge.
She took his hand, and walked with him, and seemed
The wife he sought, though shadow-like and dry.
She had one terror, lest her heart should sigh,
And tell her loudly she no longer dreamed.
She dared not say, 'This is my breast: look in.'
But there's a strength to help the desperate weak.
That night he learned how silence best can speak
The awful things when Pity pleads for Sin.
About the middle of the night her call
Was heard, and he came wondering to the bed.
'Now kiss me, dear! it may be, now!' she said.
Lethe had passed those lips, and he knew all.

L

Thus piteously Love closed what he begat:
The union of this ever-diverse pair!
These two were rapid falcons in a snare,
Condemned to do the flitting of the bat.
Lovers beneath the singing sky of May,
They wandered once; clear as the dew on flowers:
But they fed not on the advancing hours:
Their hearts held cravings for the buried day.
Then each applied to each that fatal knife,
Deep questioning, which probes to endless dole.
Ah, what a dusty answer gets the soul
When hot for certainties in this our life! —
In tragic hints here see what evermore
Moves dark as yonder midnight ocean's force,
Thundering like ramping hosts of warrior horse,
To throw that faint thin line upon the shore!

THE SAGE ENAMOURED AND THE
HONEST LADY

I

ONE fairest of the ripe unwedded left
Her shadow on the Sage's path; he found,
By common signs, that she had done a theft.
He could have made the sovereign heights resound
With questions of the wherefore of her state:
He on far other but an hour before
Intent.   And was it man, or was it mate,
That she disdained? or was there haply more?

About her mouth a placid humour slipped
The dimple, as you see smooth lakes at eve
Spread melting rings where late a swallow dipped.
The surface was attentive to receive,
The secret underneath enfolded fast.
She had the step of the unconquered, brave,
Not arrogant; and if the vessel's mast
Waved liberty, no challenge did it wave.
Her eyes were the sweet world desired of souls,
With something of a wavering line unspelt.
They held the look whose tenderness condoles
For what the sister in the look has dealt

Of fatal beyond healing; and her tones
A woman's honeyed amorous outvied,
As when in a dropped viol the wood-throb moans
Among the sobbing strings, that plain and chide
Like infants for themselves, less deep to thrill
Than those rich mother-notes for them breathed round
Those voices are not magic of the will
To strike love's wound, but of love's wound give sound
Conveying it; the yearnings, pains and dreams.
They waft to the moist tropics after storm,
When out of passion spent thick incense steams,
And jewel-belted clouds the wreck transform.
Was never hand on brush or lyre to paint
Her gracious manners, where the nuptial ring
Of melody clasped motion in restraint:
The reed-blade with the breeze thereof may sing.
With such endowments armed was she and decked
To make her spoken thoughts eclipse her kind;
Surpassing many a giant intellect,
The marvel of that cradled infant mind.
It clenched the tiny fist, it curled the toe;
Cherubic laughed, enticed, dispensed, absorbed;
And promised in fair feminine to grow
A Sage's match and mate, more heavenly orbed.

II

Across his path the spouseless Lady cast
Her shadow, and the man that thing became.
His youth uprising called his age the Past.
This was the strong grey head of laurelled name,

And in his bosom an inverted Sage
Mistook for light of morn the light which sank.
But who while veins run blood shall know the page
Succeeding ere we turn upon our blank?
Comes Beauty with her tale of moon and cloud,
Her silvered rims of mystery pointing in
To hollows of the half-veiled unavowed,
Where beats her secret life, grey heads will spin
Quick as the young, and spell those hieroglyphs
Of phosphorescent dusk devoutly bent;
They drink a cup to whirl on dizzier cliffs
For their shamed fall, which asks, why was she sent!
Why, and of whom, and whence; and tell they truth,
The legends of her mission to beguile?

Hard likeness to the toilful apes of youth,
He bore at times, and tempted the sly smile;
And not on her soft lips was it descried.
She stepped her way benevolently grave:
Nor sign that Beauty fed her worm of pride,
By tossing victim to the courtier knave,
Let peep, nor of the naughty pride gave sign.
Rather 't was humbleness in being pursued,
As pilgrim to the temple of a shrine.
Had he not wits to pierce the mask he wooed?
All wisdom's armoury this man could wield;
And if the cynic in the Sage it pleased,
Traverse her woman's curtain and poor shield,
For new example of a world diseased;
Showing her shrineless, not a temple, bare;
A curtain ripped to tatters by the blast.

Yet she most surely to this man stood fair:
He worshipped like the young enthusiast,
Named simpleton or poet.   Did he read
Right through, and with the voice she held reserved
Amid her vacant ruins jointly plead?

Compassion for the man thus noble nerved
The pity for herself she felt in him,
To wreak a deed of sacrifice, and save;
At least, be worthy.   That our soul may swim,
We sink our heart down bubbling under wave.
It bubbles till it drops among the wrecks.
But, ah! confession of a woman's breast:
She eminent, she honoured of her sex!
Truth speaks, and takes the spots of the confessed,
To veil them.   None of women, save their vile,
Plays traitor to an army in the field.
The cries most vindicating most defile.
How shall a cause to Nature be appealed,
When, under pressure of their common foe,
Her sisters shun the Mother and disown,
On pain of his intolerable crow
Above the fiction, built for him, o'erthrown?
Irrational he is, irrational
Must they be, though not Reason's light shall wane
In them with ever Nature at close call,
Behind the fiction torturing to sustain;
Who hear her in the milk, and sometimes make
A tongueless answer, shivered on a sigh:
Whereat men dread their lofty structure's quake
Once more, and in their hosts for tocsin ply

The crazy roar of peril, leonine
For injured majesty.   That sigh of dames
Is rare and soon suppressed.   Not they combine
To shake the structure sheltering them, which tames
Their lustier if not wilder : fixed are they,
In elegancy scarce denoting ease ;
And do they breathe, it is not to betray
The martyr in the caryatides.
Yet here and there along the graceful row
Is one who fetches breath from deeps, who deems,
Moved by a desperate craving, their old foe
May yield a trustier friend than woman seems,
And aid to bear the sculptured floral weight
Massed upon heads not utterly of stone :
May stamp endurance by expounding fate.
She turned to him, and, This you seek is gone ;
Look in, she said, as pants the furnace, brief,
Frost-white.   She gave his hearing sight to view
The silent chamber of a brown curled leaf :
Thing that had throbbed ere shot black lightning through.
No further sign of heart could he discern :
The picture of her speech was winter sky ;
A headless figure folding a cleft urn,
Where tears once at the overflow were dry.

III

So spake she her first utterance on the rack.
It softened torment, in the funeral hues
Round wan Romance at ebb, but drove her back
To listen to herself, herself accuse

Harshly as Love's imperial cause allowed.
She meant to grovel, and her lover praised
So high o'er the condemnatory crowd,
That she perforce a fellow phoenix blazed.

The picture was of hand fast joined to hand,
Both pushed from angry skies, their grasp more pledged
Under the threatened flash of a bright brand
At arm's length up, for severing action edged.
Why, then Love's Court of Honour contemplate;
And two drowned shorecasts, who, for the life esteemed
Above their lost, invoke an advocate
In passion's purity, thereby redeemed.

Redeemed, uplifted, glimmering on a throne,
The woman stricken by an arrow falls.
His advocate she can be, not her own,
If, Traitress to thy sex! one sister calls.

Have we such scenes of drapery's mournfulness
On Beauty's revelations, witched we plant,
Over the fair shape humbled to confess,
An angel's buckler, with loud choric chant.

                    II

No knightly sword to serve, nor harp of bard,
The lady's hand in her physician's knew.
She had not hoped for them as her award,
When zig-zag on the tongue electric flew
Her charge of counter-motives, none impure:
But muteness whipped her skin.   She could have said

Her free confession was to work his cure,
Show proofs for why she could not love or wed.
Were they not shown? His muteness shook in thrall
Her body on the verge of that black pit
Sheer from the treacherous confessional,
Demanding further, while perusing it.

Slave is the open mouth beneath the closed.
She sank; she snatched at colours; they were peel
Of fruit past savour, in derision rosed.
For the dark downward then her soul did reel.
A press of hideous impulse urged to speak:
A novel dread of man enchained her dumb.
She felt the silence thicken, heard it shriek,
Heard Life subsiding on the eternal hum:
Welcome to women, when, between man's laws
And Nature's thirsts, they, soul from body torn,
Give suck at breast to a celestial cause,
Named by the mouth infernal, and forsworn.

Nathless her forehead twitched a sad content,
To think the cure so manifest, so frail
Her charm remaining. Was the curtain's rent
Too wide? he but a man of that herd male?
She saw him as that herd of the forked head
Butting the woman harrowed on her knees,
Clothed only in life's last devouring red.
Confession at her fearful instant sees
Judicial Silence write the devil fact
In letters of the skeleton: at once,
Swayed on the supplication of her act,
The rabble reading, roaring to denounce,

She joins.   No longer colouring, with skips
At tangles, picture that for eyes in tears
Might swim the sequence, she addressed her lips
To do the scaffold's office at his ears.

Into the bitter judgement of that herd
On women, she, deeming it present, fell.
Her frenzy of abasement hugged the word
They stone with, and so pile their citadel
To launch at outcasts the foul levin bolt.
As had he flung it, in her breast it burned.
Face and reflect it did her hot revolt
From hardness, to the writhing rebel turned;
Because the golden buckler was withheld,
She to herself applies the powder-spark,
For joy of one wild demon burst ere quelled,
Perishing to astound the tyrant Dark.

She had the Scriptural word so scored on brain,
It rang through air to sky, and rocked a world
That danced down shades the scarlet dance profane;
Most women! see! by the man's view dustward hurled,
Impenitent, submissive, torn in two.
They sink upon their nature, the unnamed,
And sops of nourishment may get some few,
In place of understanding scourged and shamed.

Barely have seasoned women understood
The great Irrational, who thunders power,
Drives Nature to her primitive wild wood,
And courts her in the covert's dewy hour;

Returning to his fortress nigh night's end,
With execration of her daughters' lures.
They help him the proud fortress to defend,
Nor see what front it wears, what life immures,
The murder it commits; nor that its base
Is shifty as a huckster's opening deal
For bargain under smoothest market face,
While Gentleness bids frigid Justice feel,
Justice protests that Reason is her seat;
Elect Convenience, as Reason masked,
Hears calmly cramped Humanity entreat;
Until a sentient world is overtasked,
And rouses Reason's fountain-self: she calls
On Nature; Nature answers: Share your guilt
In common when contention cracks the walls
Of the big house which not on me is built.

The Lady said as much as breath will bear;
To happier sisters inconceivable:
Contemptible to veterans of the fair,
Who show for a convolving pearly shell,
A treasure of the shore, their written book.
As much as woman's breath will bear and live,
Shaped she to words beneath a knotted look,
That held as if for grain the summing sieve.

Her judge now brightened without pause, as wakes
Our homely daylight after dread of spells.
Lips sugared to let loose the little snakes
Of slimy lustres ringing elfin bells
About a story of the naked flesh,
Intending but to put some garment on,

Should learn, that in the subject they enmesh,
A traitor lurks and will be known anon.
Delusion heating pricks the torpid doubt,
Stationed for index down an ancient track:
And ware of it was he while she poured out,
A broken moon on forest-waters black.

Though past the stage where midway men are skilled
To scan their senses wriggling under plough,
When yet to the charmed seed of speech distilled,
Their hearts are fallow, he, and witless how,
Loathing, had yielded, like bruised limb to leech,
Not handsomely; but now beholding bleed
Soul of the woman in her prostrate speech,
The valour of that rawness he could read.
Thence flashed it, as the crimson currents ran
From senses up to thoughts, how she had read
Maternally the warm remainder man
Beneath his crust, and Nature's pity shed,
In shedding dearer than heart's blood to light
His vision of the path mild Wisdom walks.
Therewith he could espy Confession's fright:
Her need of him: these flowers grow on stalks;
They suck from soil, and have their urgencies
Beside and with the lovely face mid leaves.
Veins of divergencies, convergencies,
Our botanist in womankind perceives;
And if he hugs no wound, the man can prize
That splendid consummation and sure proof
Of more than heart in her, who might despise,
Who drowns herself, for pity up aloof

To soar and be like Nature's pity : she
Instinctive of what virtue in young days
Had served him for his pilot-star on sea,
To trouble him in haven.   Thus his gaze
Came out of rust, and more than the schooled tongue
Was gifted to encourage and assure.
He gave her of the deep well she had sprung ;
And name it gratitude, the word is poor.
But name it gratitude, is aught as rare
From sex to sex ?   And let it have survived
Their conflict, comes the peace between the pair,
Unknown to thousands husbanded and wived :
Unknown to Passion, generous for prey :
Unknown to Love, too blissful in a truce.
Their tenderest of self did each one slay ;
His cloak of dignity, her fleur de luce ;
Her lily flower, and his abolla cloak,
Things living, slew they, and no artery bled.
A moment of some sacrificial smoke,
They passed, and were the dearer for their dead.

He learnt how much we gain who make no claims.
A nightcap on his flicker of grey fire,
Was thought of her sharp shudder in the flames,
Confessing ; and its conjured image dire,
Of love, the torrent on the valley dashed ;
The whirlwind swathing tremulous peaks ; young force,
Visioned to hold corrected and abashed
Our senile emulous ; which rolls its course
Proud to the shattering end ; with these few last
Hot quintessential drops of bryony juice,

Squeezed out in anguish: all of that once vast!
And still, though having skin for man's abuse,
Though no more glorying in the beauteous wreath
Shot skyward from a blood at passionate jet,
Repenting but in words, that stand as teeth
Between the vivid lips; a vassal set;
And numb, of formal value.   Are we true
In nature, never natural thing repents;
Albeit receiving punishment for due,
Among the group of this world's penitents;
Albeit remorsefully regretting, oft
Cravenly, while the scourge no shudder spares.

Our world believes it stabler if the soft
Are whipped to show the face repentance wears.
Then hear it, in a moan of atheist gloom,
Deplore the weedy growth of hypocrites;
Count Nature devilish, and accept for doom
The chasm between our passions and our wits!

Affecting lunar whiteness, patent snows,
It trembles at betrayal of a sore.
Hers is the glacier-conscience, to expose
Impurities for clearness at the core.

She to her hungered thundering in breast,
Ye shall not starve, not feebly designates
The world repressing as a life repressed,
Judged by the wasted martyrs it creates.
How Sin, amid the shades Cimmerian,
Repents, she points for sight: and she avers,
The hoofed half-angel in the Puritan
Nigh reads her when no brutish wrath deters.

Sin against immaturity, the sin
Of ravenous excess, what deed divides
Man from vitality; these bleed within;
Bleed in the crippled relic that abides.
Perpetually they bleed; a limb is lost,
A piece of life, the very spirit maimed.
But culprit who the law of man has crossed
With Nature's, dubiously within is blamed;
Despite our cry at cutting of the whip,
Our shiver in the night when numbers frown:
We but bewail a broken fellowship,
A sting, an isolation, a fall'n crown.

Abject of sinners is that sensitive,
The flesh, amenable to stripes, miscalled
Incorrigible : such title do we give
To the poor shrinking stuff wherewith we are walled;
And taking it for Nature, place in ban
Our Mother, as a Power wanton-willed,
The shame and baffler of the soul of man,
The recreant, reptilious.   Do thou build
Thy mind on her foundations in earth's bed;
Behold man's mind the child of her keen rod,
For teaching how the wits and passions wed
To rear that temple of the credible God ;
Sacred the letters of her laws, and plain,
Will shine, to guide thy feet and hold thee firm:
Then, as a pathway through a field of grain,
Man's laws appear the blind progressive worm,
That moves by touch, and thrust of linking rings :
The which to endow with vision, lift from mud

To level of their nature's aims and springs,
Must those, the twain beside our vital flood,
Now on opposing banks, the twain at strife
(Whom the so rosy ferryman invites
To junction, and mid-channel over Life,
Unmasked to the ghostly, much asunder smites),
Instruct in deeper than Convenience,
In higher than the harvest of a year.
Only the rooted knowledge to high sense
Of heavenly can mount, and feel the spur
For fruitfullest advancement, eye a mark
Beyond the path with grain on either hand,
Help to the steering of our social Ark
Over the barbarous waters unto land.

For us the double conscience and its war,
The serving of two masters, false to both,
Until those twain, who spring the root and are
The knowledge in division, plight a troth
Of equal hands: nor longer circulate
A pious token for their current coin,
To growl at the exchange; they, mate and mate,
Fair feminine and masculine shall join
Upon an upper plane, still common mould,
Where stamped religion and reflective pace
A statelier measure, and the hoop of gold
Rounds to horizon for their soul's embrace.
Then shall those noblest of the earth and sun
Inmix unlike to waves on savage sea.
But not till Nature's laws and man's are one.
Can marriage of the man and woman be.

v

He passed her through the sermon's dull defile.
Down under billowy vapour-gorges heaved
The city and the vale and mountain-pile.
She felt strange push of shuttle-threads that weaved.

A new land in an old beneath her lay;
And forth to meet it did her spirit rush,
As bride who without shame has come to say,
Husband, in his dear face that caused her blush.

A natural woman's heart, not more than clad
By station and bright raiment, gathers heat
From nakedness in trusted hands : she had
The joy of those who feel the world's heart beat,
After long doubt of it as fire or ice ;
Because one man had helped her to breathe free ;
Surprised to faith in something of a price
Past the old charity in chivalry : —
Our first wild step to right the loaded scales
Displaying women shamefully outweighed.
The wisdom of humaneness best avails
For serving justice till that fraud is brayed.

Her buried body fed the life she drank.
And not another stripping of her wound !
The startled thought on black delirium sank,
While with her gentle surgeon she communed,

And woman's prospect of the yoke repelled.
Her buried body gave her flowers and food;
The peace, the homely skies, the springs that welled;
Love, the large love that folds the multitude.

Soul's chastity in honesty, and this
With beauty, made the dower to men refused.
And little do they know the prize they miss;
Which is their happy fortune!   Thus he mused.

For him, the cynic in the Sage had play
A hazy moment, by a breath dispersed;
To think, of all alive most wedded they,
Whom time disjoined!   He needed her quick thirst
For renovated earth: on earth she gazed,
With humble aim to foot beside the wise.
Lo, where the eyelashes of night are raised
Yet lowly over morning's pure grey eyes.

LOVE IS WINGED

Love is winged for two,
In the worst he weathers,
When their hearts are tied;
But if they divide,
O too true!
Cracks a globe, and feathers, feathers,
Feathers all the ground bestrew.

I was breast of morning sea,
Rosy plume on forest dun,
I the laugh in rainy fleeces,
While with me
She made one.
Now must we pick up our pieces,
For that then so winged were we

ASK, IS LOVE DIVINE

Ask, is Love divine,
Voices all are, ay.
Question for the sign,
There 's a common sigh.
Would we through our years,
Love forego,
Quit of scars and tears?
Ah, but no, no, no!

JOY IS FLEET

Joy is fleet,
Sorrow slow.
Love so sweet,
Sorrow will sow.
Love, that has flown
Ere day's decline,
Love to have known,
Sorrow, be mine!

THE LESSON OF GRIEF

Not ere the bitter herb we taste,
Which ages thought of happy times,
To plant us in a weeping waste,
Rings with our fellows this one heart
         Accordant chimes.

When I had shed my glad year's leaf,
I did believe I stood alone,
Till that great company of Grief
Taught me to know this craving heart
         For not my own.

THE WOODS OF WESTERMAIN

I

ENTER these enchanted woods,
    You who dare.
Nothing harms beneath the leaves
More than waves a swimmer cleaves.
Toss your heart up with the lark,
Foot at peace with mouse and worm,
    Fair you fare.
Only at a dread of dark
Quaver, and they quit their form:
Thousand eyeballs under hoods
    Have you by the hair.
Enter these enchanted woods,
    You who dare.

II

Here the snake across your path
Stretches in his golden bath:
Mossy-footed squirrels leap
Soft as winnowing plumes of Sleep:
Yaffles on a chuckle skim
Low to laugh from branches dim:
Up the pine, where sits the star,
Rattles deep the moth-winged jar.

Each has business of his own ;
But should you distrust a tone,
    Then beware.
Shudder all the haunted roods,
All the eyeballs under hoods
    Shroud you in their glare.
Enter these enchanted woods,
    You who dare.

III

Open hither, open hence,
Scarce a bramble weaves a fence,
Where the strawberry runs red,
With white star-flower overhead ;
Cumbered by dry twig and cone,
Shredded husks of seedlings flown,
Mine of mole and spotted flint :
Of dire wizardry no hint,
Save mayhap the print that shows
Hasty outward-tripping toes,
Heels to terror, on the mould.
These, the woods of Westermain,
Are as others to behold,
Rich of wreathing sun and rain ;
Foliage lustreful around
Shadowed leagues of slumbering sound.
Wavy tree-tops, yellow whins,
Shelter eager minikins,
Myriads, free to peck and pipe :
Would you better ? would you worse ?

You with them may gather ripe
Pleasures flowing not from purse.
Quick and far as Colour flies
Taking the delighted eyes,
You of any well that springs
May unfold the heaven of things;
Have it homely and within,
And thereof its likeness win,
Will you so in soul's desire:
This do sages grant t' the lyre.
This is being bird and more,
More than glad musician this;
Granaries you will have a store
Past the world of woe and bliss;
Sharing still its bliss and woe;
Harnessed to its hungers, no.
On the throne Success usurps,
You shall seat the joy you feel
Where a race of water chirps,
Twisting hues of flourished steel:
Or where light is caught in hoop
Up a clearing's leafy rise,
Where the crossing deerherds troop
Classic splendours, knightly dyes.
Or, where old-eyed oxen chew
Speculation with the cud,
Read their pool of vision through,
Back to hours when mind was mud;
Nigh the knot, which did untwine
Timelessly to drowsy suns;
Seeing Earth a slimy spine,

Heaven a space for winging tons.
Farther, deeper, may you read,
Have you sight for things afield,
Where peeps she, the Nurse of seed,
Cloaked, but in the peep revealed;
Showing a kind face and sweet:
Look you with the soul you see't.
Glory narrowing to grace,
Grace to glory magnified,
Following that will you embrace
Close in arms or aëry wide.
Banished is the white Foam-born
Not from here, nor under ban
Phoebus lyrist, Phoebe's horn,
Pipings of the reedy Pan.
Loved of Earth of old they were,
Loving did interpret her;
And the sterner worship bars
None whom Song has made her stars.
You have seen the huntress moon
Radiantly facing dawn,
Dusky meads between them strewn
Glimmering like downy awn:
Argent Westward glows the hunt,
East the blush about to climb;
One another fair they front,
Transient, yet outshine the time;
Even as dewlight off the rose
In the mind a jewel sows.
Thus opposing grandeurs live
Here if Beauty be their dower:

Doth she of her spirit give,
Fleetingness will spare her flower.
This is in the tune we play,
Which no spring of strength would quell;
In subduing does not slay;
Guides the channel, guards the well:
Tempered holds the young blood-heat,
Yet through measured grave accord,
Hears the heart of wildness beat
Like a centaur's hoof on sward.
Drink the sense the notes infuse,
You a larger self will find:
Sweetest fellowship ensues
With the creatures of your kind.
Ay, and Love, if Love it be
Flaming over *I* and *ME*,
Love meet they who do not shove
Cravings in the van of Love.
Courtly dames are here to woo,
Knowing love if it be true.
Reverence the blossom-shoot
Fervently, they are the fruit.
Mark them stepping, hear them talk,
Goddess, is no myth inane,
You will say of those who walk
In the woods of Westermain.
Waters that from throat and thigh
Dart the sun his arrows back;
Leaves that on a woodland sigh
Chat of secret things no lack;
Shadowy branch-leaves, waters clear.

Bare or veiled they move sincere;
Not by slavish terrors tripped;
Being anew in nature dipped,
Growths of what they step on, these;
With the roots the grace of trees.
Casket-breasts they give, nor hide,
For a tyrant's flattered pride,
Mind, which nourished not by light,
Lurks the shuffling trickster sprite:
Whereof are strange tales to tell;
Some in blood writ, tombed in bell.
Here the ancient battle ends,
Joining two astonished friends,
Who the kiss can give and take
With more warmth than in that world
Where the tiger claws the snake,
Snake her tiger clasps infurled,
And the issue of their fight
Peoples lands in snarling plight.
Here her splendid beast she leads
Silken-leashed and decked with weeds
Wild as he, but breathing faint
Sweetness of unfelt constraint.
Love, the great volcano, flings
Fires of lower Earth to sky;
Love, the sole permitted, sings
Sovereignly of *ME* and *I*.
Bowers he has of sacred shade,
Spaces of superb parade,
Voiceful . . . But bring you a note
Wrangling, howsoe'er remote,

Discords out of discord spin
Round and round derisive din:
Sudden will a pallor pant
Chill at screeches miscreant;
Owls or spectres, thick they flee;
Nightmare upon horror broods;
Hooded laughter, monkish glee,
    Gaps the vital air.
Enter these enchanted woods
    You who dare.

IV

You must love the light so well
That no darkness will seem fell.
Love it so you could accost
Fellowly a livid ghost.
Whish! the phantom wisps away,
Owns him smoke to cocks of day.
In your breast the light must burn
Fed of you, like corn in quern
Ever plumping while the wheel
Speeds the mill and drains the meal.
Light to light sees little strange,
Only features heavenly new;
Then you touch the nerve of Change,
Then of Earth you have the clue;
Then her two-sexed meanings melt
Through you, wed the thought and felt.
Sameness locks no scurfy pond
Here for Custom, crazy-fond:

Change is on the wing to bud
Rose in brain from rose in blood.
Wisdom throbbing shall you see
Central in complexity;
From her pasture 'mid the beasts
Rise to her ethereal feasts,
Not, though lightnings track your wit
Starward, scorning them you quit:
For be sure the bravest wing
Preens it in our common spring,
Thence along the vault to soar,
You with others, gathering more,
Glad of more, till you reject
Your proud title of elect,
Perilous even here while few
Roam the arched greenwood with you.
      Heed that snare.
Muffled by his cavern-cowl
Squats the scaly Dragon-fowl,
Who was lord ere light you drank,
And lest blood of knightly rank
Stream, let not your fair princess
Stray: he holds the leagues in stress,
      Watches keenly there.
Oft has he been riven; slain
Is no force in Westermain.
Wait, and we shall forge him curbs,
Put his fangs to uses, tame,
Teach him, quick as cunning herbs,
How to cure him sick and lame.
Much restricted, much enringed,

Much he frets, the hooked and winged,
    Never known to spare.
'T is enough: the name of Sage
Hits no thing in nature, nought;
Man the least, save when grave Age
From yon Dragon guards his thought.
Eye him when you hearken dumb
To what words from Wisdom come.
When she says how few are by
Listening to her, eye his eye.
    Self, his name declare.
Him shall Change, transforming late,
Wonderously renovate.
Hug himself the creature may:
What he hugs is loathed decay.
Crying, slip thy scales, and slough!
Change will strip his armour off;
Make of him who was all maw,
Inly only thrilling-shrewd,
Such a servant as none saw
Through his days of dragonhood.
Days when growling o'er his bone,
Sharpened he for mine and thine;
Sensitive within alone;
Scaly as in clefts of pine.
Change, the strongest son of Life,
Has the Spirit here to wife.
Lo, their young of vivid breed,
Bear the lights that onward speed,
Threading thickets, mounting glades,
Up the verdurous colonnades,

Round the fluttered curves, and down,
Out of sight of Earth's blue crown,
Whither, in her central space,
Spouts the Fount and Lure o' the chase.
Fount unresting, Lure divine!
There meet all: too late look most.
Fire in water hued as wine,
Springs amid a shadowy host;
Circled: one close-headed mob,
Breathless, scanning divers heaps
Where a Heart begins to throb,
Where it ceases, slow, with leaps.
And 't is very strange, 't is said,
How you spy in each of them
Semblance of that Dragon red,
As the oak in bracken-stem.
And, 't is said, how each and each:
Which commences, which subsides:
First my Dragon! doth beseech
Her who food for all provides.
And she answers with no sign;
Utters neither yea nor nay;
Fires the water hued as wine;
Kneads another spark in clay.
Terror is about her hid;
Silence of the thunders locked;
Lightnings lining the shut lid;
Fixity on quaking rocked.
Lo, you look at Flow and Drought
Interflashed and interwrought:
Ended is begun, begun

Ended, quick as torrents run.
Young Impulsion spouts to sink;
Luridness and lustre link;
'T is your come and go of breath;
Mirrored pants the Life, the Death;
Each of either reaped and sown:
Rosiest rosy wanes to crone.
See you so? your senses drift;
'T is a shuttle weaving swift.
Look with spirit past the sense,
Spirit shines in permanence.
That is She, the view of whom
Is the dust within the tomb,
Is the inner blush above,
Look to loathe, or look to love;
Think her Lump, or know her Flame;
Dread her scourge, or read her aim;
Shoot your hungers from their nerve;
Or, in her example, serve.
Some have found her sitting grave;
Laughing, some; or, browed with sweat,
Hurling dust of fool and knave
In a hissing smithy's jet.
More it were not well to speak;
Burn to see, you need but seek.
Once beheld she gives the key
Airing every doorway, she.
Little can you stop or steer
Ere of her you are the seër.
On the surface she will witch,
Rendering Beauty yours, but gaze

Under, and the soul is rich
Past computing, past amaze.
Then is courage that endures
Even her awful tremble yours.
Then, the reflex of that Fount
Spied below, will Reason mount
Lordly and a quenchless force,
Lighting Pain to its mad source,
Scaring Fear till Fear escapes,
Shot through all its phantom shapes.
Then your spirit will perceive
Fleshly seed of fleshly sins;
Where the passions interweave,
How the serpent tangle spins
Of the sense of Earth misprised,
Brainlessly unrecognized;
She being Spirit in her clods,
Footway to the God of Gods.
Then for you are pleasures pure,
Sureties as the stars are sure:
Not the wanton beckoning flags
Which, of flattery and delight,
Wax to the grim Habit-Hags
Riding souls of men to night:
Pleasures that through blood run sane,
Quickening spirit from the brain.
Each of each in sequent birth,
Blood and brain and spirit, three
(Say the deepest gnomes of Earth),
Join for true felicity.
Are they parted, then expect

Some one sailing will be wrecked:
Separate hunting are they sped,
Scan the morsel coveted.
Earth that Triad is: she hides
Joy from him who that divides;
Showers it when the three are one ·
Glassing her in union.
Earth your haven, Earth your helm,
You command a double realm:
Labouring here to pay your debt,
Till your little sun shall set;
Leaving her the future task:
Loving her too well to ask.
Eglantine that climbs the yew,
She her darkest wreathes for those
Knowing her the Ever-new,
And themselves the kin o' the rose.
Life, the chisel, axe and sword,
Wield who have her depths explored:
Life, the dream, shall be their robe, .
Large as air about the globe;
Life, the question, hear its cry
Echoed with concordant Why;
Life, the small self-dragon ramped
Thrill for service to be stamped.
Ay, and over every height
Life for them shall wave a wand:
That, the last, where sits affright,
Homely shows the stream beyond.
Love the light and be its lynx,
You will track her and attain;

Read her as no cruel Sphinx
In the woods of Westermain.

Daily fresh the woods are ranged;
Glooms which otherwhere appal,
Sounded: here, their worths exchanged,
Urban joins with pastoral:
Little lost, save what may drop
Husk-like, and the mind preserves.
Natural overgrowths they lop,
Yet from nature neither swerves,
Trained or savage: for this cause:
Of our Earth they ply the laws,
Have in Earth their feeding root,
Mind of man and bent of brute.
Hear that song; both wild and ruled.
Hear it: is it wail or mirth?
Ordered, bubbled, quite unschooled?
None, and all: it springs of Earth.
O but hear it! 't is the mind;
Mind that with deep Earth unites,
Round the solid trunk to wind
Rings of clasping parasites.
Music have you there to feed
Simplest and most soaring need.
Free to wind, and in desire
Winding, they to her attached
Feel the trunk a spring of fire,
And ascend to heights unmatched,
Whence the tidal world is viewed
As a sea of windy wheat,
Momently black, barren, rude;

Golden-brown, for harvest meet;
Dragon-reaped from folly-sown;
Bride-like to the sickle-blade:
Quick it varies, while the moan,
Moan of a sad creature strayed,
Chiefly is its voice.   So flesh
Conjures tempest-flails to thresh
Good from worthless.   Some clear lamps
Light it; more of dead marsh-damps.
Monster is it still, and blind,
Fit but to be led by Pain.
Glance we at the paths behind,
Fruitful sight has Westermain.
There we laboured, and in turn
Forward our blown lamps discern,
As you see on the dark deep
Far the loftier billows leap,
    Foam for beacon bear.
Hither, hither, if you will,
Drink instruction, or instil,
Run the woods like vernal sap,
Crying, hail to luminousness!
    But have care.
In yourself may lurk the trap:
On conditions they caress.
Here you meet the light invoked:
Here is never secret cloaked.
Doubt you with the monster's **fry**
All his orbit may exclude;
Are you of the stiff, the dry,
Cursing the not understood;

Grasp you with the monster's claws;
Govern with his truncheon-saws;
Hate, the shadow of a grain;
You are lost in Westermain:
Earthward swoops a vulture sun,
Nighted upon carrion:
Straightway venom winecups shout
Toasts to One whose eyes are out:
Flowers along the reeling floor
Drip henbane and hellebore:
Beauty, of her tresses shorn,
Shrieks as nature's maniac:
Hideousness on hoof and horn
Tumbles, yapping in her track:
Haggard Wisdom, stately once,
Leers fantastical and trips:
Allegory drums the sconce,
Impiousness nibblenips.
Imp that dances, imp that flits,
Imp o' the demon-growing girl,
Maddest! whirl with imp o' the pits
Round you, and with them you whirl
Fast where pours the fountain-rout
Out of Him whose eyes are out:
Multitudes on multitudes,
Drenched in wallowing devilry:
And you ask where you may be,
    In what reek of a lair
Given to bones and ogre-broods:
    And they yell you Where.
Enter these enchanted woods,
    You who dare.

A BALLAD OF PAST MERIDIAN

I

LAST night returning from my twilight walk
I met the grey mist Death, whose eyeless brow
Was bent on me, and from his hand of chalk
He reached me flowers as from a withered bough:
O Death, what bitter nosegays givest thou!

II

Death said, I gather, and pursued his way.
Another stood by me, a shape in stone,
Sword-hacked and iron-stained, with breasts of clay,
And metal veins that sometimes fiery shone:
O Life, how naked and how hard when known!

III

Life said, As thou hast carved me, such am I.
Then memory, like the nightjar on the pine,
And sightless hope, a woodlark in night sky,
Joined notes of Death and Life till night's decline
Of Death, of Life, those inwound notes are mine.

THE DAY OF THE DAUGHTER OF HADES

I

He who has looked upon Earth
Deeper than flower and fruit,
Losing some hue of his mirth,
As the tree striking rock at the root,
Unto him shall the marvellous tale
Of Callistes more humanly come
With the touch on his breast than a hail
    From the markets that hum.

II

Now the youth footed swift to the dawn.
'T was the season when wintertide,
In the higher rock-hollows updrawn,
Leaves meadows to bud, and he spied,
By light throwing shallow shade,
Between the beam and the gloom,
Sicilian Enna, whose Maid
Such aspect wears in her bloom
Underneath since the Charioteer
Of Darkness whirled her away,
On a reaped afternoon of the year,
Nigh the poppy-droop of Day.

O and naked of her, all dust,
The majestic Mother and Nurse,
Ringing cries to the God, the Just,
Curled the land with the blight of her curse:
Recollected of this glad isle
Still quaking.   But now more fair,
And momently fraying the while
The veil of the shadows there,
Soft Enna that prostrate grief
Sang through, and revealed round the vines,
Bronze-orange, the crisp young leaf,
The wheat-blades tripping in lines,
A hue unillumined by sun
Of the flowers flooding grass as from founts:
All the penetrable dun
     Of the morn ere she mounts.

III

Nor had saffron and sapphire and red
Waved aloft to their sisters below,
When gaped by the rock-channel head
Of the lake, black, a cave at one blow,
Reverberant over the plain:
A sound oft fearfully swung
For the coming of wrathful rain:
And forth, like the dragon-tongue
Of a fire beaten flat by the gale,
But more as the smoke to behold,
A chariot burst.   Then a wail
Quivered high of the love that would fold

Bliss immeasurable, bigger than heart,
Though a God's: and the wheels were stayed,
And the team of the chariot swart
Reared in marble, the six, dismayed,
Like hoofs that by night plashing sea
Curve and ramp from the vast swan-wave:
For, lo, the Great Mother, She!
And Callistes gazed, he gave
His eyeballs up to the sight:
The embrace of the Twain, of whom
To men are their day, their night,
Mellow fruits and the shearing tomb:
Our Lady of the Sheaves
And the Lily of Hades, the Sweet
Of Enna: he saw through leaves
The Mother and Daughter meet.
They stood by the chariot-wheel,
Embraced, very tall, most like
Fellow poplars, wind-taken, that reel
Down their shivering columns and strike
Head to head, crossing throats: and apart,
For the feast of the look, they drew,
Which Darkness no longer could thwart;
And they broke together anew,
Exulting to tears, flower and bud.
But the mate of the Rayless was grave:
She smiled like Sleep on its flood,
That washes of all we crave:
Like the trance of eyes awake
And the spirit enshrouded, she cast
The wan underworld on the lake.
    They were so and they passed.

IV

He tells it, who knew the law
Upon mortals : he stood alive
Declaring that this he saw:
        He could see, and survive.

V

Now the youth was not ware of the beams
With the grasses intertwined,
For each thing seen, as in dreams,
Came stepping to rear through his mind,
Till it struck his remembered prayer
To be witness of this which had flown
Like a smoke melted thinner than air,
That the vacancy doth disown.
And viewing a maiden, he thought
It might now be morn, and afar
Within him the memory wrought
Of a something that slipped from the car
When those, the august, moved by :
Perchance a scarf, and perchance
This maiden.   She did not fly,
Nor started at his advance :
She looked, as when infinite thirst
Pants pausing to bless the springs,
Refreshed, unsated.   Then first
He trembled with awe of the things

He had seen; and he did transfer,
Divining and doubting in turn,
His reverence unto her;
Nor asked what he crouched to learn:
The whence of her, whither, and why
Her presence there, and her name,
Her parentage: under which sky
Her birth, and how hither she came,
So young, a virgin, alone,
Unfriended, having no fear,
As Oreads have; no moan,
Like the lost upon earth; no tear;
Not a sign of the torch in the blood,
Though her stature had reached the height
When mantles a tender rud
In maids that of youths have sight,
If maids of our seed they be:
For he said: A glad vision art thou!
And she answered him: Thou to me!
    As men utter a vow.

VI

Then said she, quick as the cries
Of the rainy cranes: Light! light!
And Helios rose in her eyes,
That were full as the dew-balls bright,
Relucent to him as dews
Unshaded. Breathing, she sent
Her voice to the God of the Muse,
And along the vale it went,

Strange to hear: not thin, not shrill:
Sweet, but no young maid's throat:
The echo beyond the hill
Ran falling on half the note:
And under the shaken ground
Where the Hundred-headed groans
By the roots of great Ætna bound,
As of him were hollow tones
Of wondering roared: a tale
Repeated to sunless halls.
But now off the face of the vale
Shadows fled in a breath, and the walls
Of the lake's rock-head were gold,
And the breast of the lake, that swell
Of the crestless long wave rolled
To shore-bubble, pebble and shell.
A morning of radiant lids
O'er the dance of the earth opened wide:
The bees chose their flowers, the snub kids
Upon hindlegs went sportive, or plied,
Nosing, hard at the dugs to be filled:
There was milk, honey, music to make:
Up their branches the little birds billed:
Chirrup, drone, bleat and buzz ringed the lake.
O shining in sunlight, chief
After water and water's caress,
Was the young bronze-orange leaf,
That clung to the tree as a tress,
Shooting lucid tendrils to wed
With the vine-hook tree or pole,
Like Arachne launched out on her thread.

Then the maiden her dusky stole
In the span of the black-starred zone,
Gathered up for her footing fleet.
As one that had toil of her own
She followed the lines of wheat
Tripping straight through the field, green blades,
To the groves of olive grey,
Downy-grey, golden-tinged: and to glades
Where the pear-blossom thickens the spray
In a night, like the snow-packed storm:
Pear, apple, almond, plum:
Not wintry now: pushing, warm!
And she touched them with finger and thumb,
As the vine-hook closes: she smiled,
Recounting again and again,
Corn, wine, fruit, oil! like a child,
With the meaning known to men.
For hours in the track of the plough
And the pruning-knife she stepped,
And of how the seed works, and of how
Yields the soil, she seemed adept.
Then she murmured that name of the dearth,
The Beneficent, Hers, who bade
Our husbandmen sow for the birth
Of the grain making earth full glad.
She murmured that Other's: the dirge
Of life-light: for whose dark lap
Our locks are clipped on the verge
Of the realm where runs no sap.
She said: We have looked on both!
And her eyes had a wavering beam

Of various lights, like the froth
Of the storm-swollen ravine stream
In flame of the bolt.   What links
Were these which had made him her friend?
He eyed her, as one who drinks,
    And would drink to the end.

VII

Now the meadows with crocus besprent,
And the asphodel woodsides she left,
And the lake-slopes, the ravishing scent
Of narcissus, dark-sweet, for the cleft
That tutors the torrent-brook,
Delaying its forceful spleen
With many a wind and crook
Through rock to the broad ravine.
By the hyacinth-bells in the brakes,
And the shade-loved white windflower, half hid,
And the sun-loving lizards and snakes
On the cleft's barren ledges, that slid
Out of sight, smooth as waterdrops, all,
At a snap of twig or bark
In the track of the foreign foot-fall,
She climbed to the pineforest dark,
Overbrowing an emerald chine
Of the glass-billows.   Thence, as a wreath,
Running poplar and cypress to pine,
The lake-banks are seen, and beneath,
Vineyard, village, groves, rivers, towers, farms,
The citadel watching the bay,

The bay with the town in its arms,
The town shining white as the spray
Of the sapphire sea-wave on the rock,
Where the rock stars the girdle of sea,
White-ringed, as the midday flock,
Clipped by heat, rings the round of the tree
That hour of the piercing shaft
Transfixes bough-shadows, confused
In veins of fire, and she laughed,
With her quiet mouth amused,
To see the whole flock, adroop,
Asleep, hug the tree-stem as one,
Imperceptibly filling the loop
Of its shade at a slant of sun.
The pipes under pent of the crag,
Where the goatherds in piping recline,
Have whimsical stops, burst and flag
Uncorrected as outstretched swine :
For the fingers are slack and unsure,
And the wind issues querulous : — thorns
And snakes ! — but she listened demure,
Comparing day's music with morn's.
Of the gentle spirit that slips
From the bark of the tree she discoursed,
And of her of the wells, whose lips
Are coolness enchanting, rock-sourced.
And much of the sacred loon,
The frolic, the Goatfoot God,
For stories of indolent noon
In the pineforest's odorous nod,
She questioned, not knowing : he can

Be waspish, irascible, rude,
He is oftener friendly to man,
And ever to beasts and their brood.
For the which did she love him well,
She said, and his pipes of the reed,
His twitched lips puffing to tell
In music his tears and his need,
Against the sharp catch of his hurt.
Not as shepherds of Pan did she speak,
Nor spake as the schools, to divert,
But fondly, perceiving him weak
Before Gods, and to shepherds a fear,
A holiness, horn and heel.
All this she had learnt in her ear
From Callistes, and taught him to feel.
Yea, the solemn divinity flushed
Through the shaggy brown skin of the beast,
And the steeps where the cataract rushed,
And the wilds where the forest is priest,
Were his temple to clothe him in awe,
While she spake : 't was a wonder : she read
The haunts of the beak and the claw
As plain as the land of bread,
But Cities and martial States,
Whither soon the youth veered his theme,
Were impervious barrier-gates
To her : and that ship, a trireme,
Nearing harbour, scarce wakened her glance,
Though he dwelt on the message it bore
Of sceptre and sword and lance
To the bee-swarms black on the shore,

Which were audible almost,
So black they were.   It befell
That he called up the warrior host
Of the Song pouring hydromel
In thunder, the wide-winged Song.
And he named with his boyish pride
The heroes, the noble throng
Past Acheron now, foul tide!
With his joy of the godlike band
And the verse divine, he named
The chiefs pressing hot on the strand,
Seen of Gods, of Gods aided, and maimed.
The fleetfoot and ireful; the King;
Him, the prompter in stratagem,
Many-shifted and masterful: Sing,
O Muse! But she cried: Not of them!
She breathed as if breath had failed,
And her eyes, while she bade him desist,
Held the lost-to-light ghosts grey-mailed,
As you see the grey river-mist
Hold shapes on the yonder bank.
A moment her body waned,
The light of her sprang and sank:
Then she looked at the sun, she regained
Clear feature, and she breathed deep.
She wore the wan smile he had seen,
As the flow of the river of Sleep,
On the mouth of the Shadow-Queen.
In sunlight she craved to bask,
Saying: Life!   And who was she? who?
Of what issue?   He dared not ask,
        For that partly he knew.

VIII

A noise of the hollow ground
Turned the eye to the ear in debate:
Not the soft overflowing of sound
Of the pines, ranked, lofty, straight,
Barely swayed to some whispers remote,
Some swarming whispers above:
Not the pines with the faint airs afloat,
Hush-hushing the nested dove:
It was not the pines, or the rout
Oft heard from mid-forest in chase,
But the long muffled roar of a shout
Subterranean.   Sharp grew her face.
She rose, yet not moved by affright;
'T was rather good haste to use
Her holiday of delight
In the beams of the God of the Muse.
And the steeps of the forest she crossed,
On its dry red sheddings and cones
Up the paths by roots green-mossed,
Spotted amber, and old mossed stones.
Then out where the brook-torrent starts
To her leap, and from bend to curve
A hurrying elbow darts
For the instant-glancing swerve,
Decisive, with violent will
In the action formed, like hers,
The maiden's, ascending; and still
Ascending, the bud of the furze,
The broom, and all blue-berried shoots

Of stubborn and prickly kind,
The juniper flat on its roots,
The dwarf rhododaphne, behind
She left, and the mountain sheep
Far behind, goat, herbage and flower.
The island was hers, and the deep,
All heaven, a golden hour.
Then with wonderful voice that rang
Through air as the swan's nigh death,
Of the glory of Light she sang,
She sang of the rapture of Breath.
Nor ever, says he who heard,
Heard Earth in her boundaries broad,
From bosom of singer or bird
A sweetness thus rich of the God
Whose harmonies always are sane.
She sang of furrow and seed,
The burial, birth of the grain,
The growth, and the showers that feed,
And the green blades waxing mature
For the husbandman's armful brown.
O, the song in its burden ran pure,
And burden to song was a crown.
Callistes, a singer, skilled
In the gift he could measure and praise,
By a rival's art was thrilled,
Though she sang but a Song of Days,
Where the husbandman's toil and strife
Little varies to strife and toil:
But the milky kernel of life,
With her numbered : corn, wine, fruit, oil!

The song did give him to eat:
Gave the first rapt vision of Good,
And the fresh young sense of Sweet:
The grace of the battle for food,
With the issue Earth cannot refuse
When men to their labour are sworn.
'T was a song of the God of the Muse
　　To the forehead of Morn.

IX

Him loved she.　Lo, now was he veiled:
Over sea stood a swelled cloud-rack:
The fishing-boat havenward sailed,
Bent abeam with a whitened track,
Surprised, fast hauling the net,
As it flew : sea dashed, earth shook.
She said : Is it night ?　O not yet !
With a travail of thoughts in her look.
The mountain heaved up to its peak :
Sea darkened : earth gathered her fowl :
Of bird or of branch rose the shriek.
Night ? but never so fell a scowl
Wore night, nor the sky since then
When ocean ran swallowing shore,
And the Gods looked down for men.
Broke tempest with that stern roar
Never yet, save when black on the whirl
Rode wrath of a sovereign Power.
Then the youth and the shuddering girl,
Dim as shades in the angry shower,

Joined hands and descended a maze
Of the paths that were racing alive
Round boulder and bush, cleaving ways,
Incessant, with sound of a hive.
The height was a fountain-urn
Pouring streams, and the whole solid height
Leaped, chasing at every turn
The pair in one spirit of flight
To the folding pineforest.   Yet here,
Like the pause to things hunted, in doubt,
The stillness bred spectral fear
Of the awfulness ranging without,
And imminent.   Downward they fled,
From under the haunted roof,
To the valley aquake with the tread
Of an iron-resounding hoof,
As of legions of thunderful horse
Broken loose and in line tramping hard.
For the rage of a hungry force
Roamed blind of its mark over sward:
They saw it rush dense in the cloak
Of its travelling swathe of steam,
All the vale through a thin thread-smoke
Was thrown back to distance extreme:
And dull the full breast of it blinked,
Like a buckler of steel breathed o'er,
Diminished, in strangeness distinct,
Glowing cold, unearthly, hoar:
An Enna of fields beyond sun,
Out of light, in a lurid web,
And the traversing fury spun

Up and down with a wave's flow and ebb;
As the wave breaks to grasp and to spurn,
Retire, and in ravenous greed,
Inveterate, swell its return.
Up and down, as if wringing from speed
Sights that made the unsighted appear,
Delude and dissolve, on it scoured.
Lo, a sea upon land held career
Through the plain of the vale half-devoured.
Callistes of home and escape
Muttered swiftly, unwitting of speech.
She gazed at the Void of shape,
She put her white hand to his reach,
Saying: Now have we looked on the Three.
And divided from day, from night,
From air that is breath, stood she,
      Like the vale, out of light.

x

Then again in disorderly words
He muttered of home, and was mute,
With the heart of the cowering birds
Ere they burst off the fowler's foot.
He gave her some redness that streamed
Through her limbs in a flitting glow.
The sigh of our life she seemed,
The bliss of it clothing in woe.
Frailer than flower when the round
Of the sickle encircles it: strong
To tell of the things profound,

Our inmost uttering song,
Unspoken.   So stood she awhile
In the gloom of the terror afield,
And the silence about her smile
Said more than of tongue is revealed.
I have breathed: I have gazed: I have been:
It said: and not joylessly shone
The remembrance of light through the screen
Of a face that seemed shadow and stone.
She led the youth trembling, appalled,
To the lake-banks he saw sink and rise
Like a panic-struck breast.   Then she called,
And the hurricane blackness had eyes.
It launched like the Thunderer's bolt.
Pale she drooped, and the youth by her side
Would have clasped her and dared a revolt
Sacrilegious as ever defied
High Olympus, but vainly for strength
His compassionate heart shook a frame
Stricken rigid to ice all its length.
On amain the black traveller came.
Lo, a chariot, cleaving the storm,
Clove the fountaining lake with a plough,
And the lord of the steeds was in form
He, the God of implacable brow,
Darkness: he: he in person: he raged
Through the wave like a boar of the wilds
From the hunters and hounds disengaged,
And a name shouted hoarsely: his child's.
Horror melted in anguish to hear.
Lo, the wave hissed apart for the path

Of the terrible Charioteer,
With the foam and torn features of wrath,
Hurled aloft on each arm in a sheet;
And the steeds clove it, rushing at land
Like the teeth of the famished at meat.
    Then he swept out his hand.

XI

This, no more, doth Callistes recall:
He saw, ere he dropped in swoon,
On the maiden the chariot fall,
As a thundercloud swings on the moon.
Forth, free of the deluge, one cry
From the vanishing gallop rose clear:
And: Skiágeneia! the sky
Rang: Skiágeneia! the sphere.
And she left him therewith, to rejoice,
Repine, yearn, and know not his aim,
The life of their day in her voice,
    Left her life in her name.

XII

Now the valley in ruin of fields
And fair meadowland, showing at eve
Like the spear-pitted warrior's shields
After battle, bade men believe
That no other than wrathfullest God
Had been loose on her beautiful breast,

Where the flowery grass was clod,
Wheat and vine as a trailing nest.
The valley, discreet in grief,
Disclosed but the open truth,
And Enna had hope of the sheaf:
There was none for the desolate youth
Devoted to mourn and to crave.
Of the secret he had divined
Of his friend of a day would he rave:
How for light of our earth she pined:
For the olive, the vine and the wheat,
Burning through with inherited fire:
And when Mother went Mother to meet,
She was prompted by simple desire
In the day-destined car to have place
At the skirts of the Goddess, unseen,
And be drawn to the dear earth's face.
She was fire for the blue and the green
Of our earth, dark fire; athirst
As a seed of her bosom for dawn,
White air that had robed and nursed
Her mother.   Now was she gone
With the Silent, the God without tear,
Like a bud peeping out of its sheath
To be sundered and stamped with the sere.
And Callistes to her beneath,
As she to our beams, extinct,
Strained arms: he was shade of her shade.
In division so were they linked.
But the song which had betrayed
Her flight to the cavernous ear

For its own keenly wakeful: that song
Of the sowing and reaping, and cheer
Of the husbandman's heart made strong
Through droughts and deluging rains
With his faith in the Great Mother's love:
O the joy of the breath she sustains,
And the lyre of the light above,
And the first rapt vision of Good,
And the fresh young sense of Sweet:
That song the youth ever pursued
In the track of her footing fleet.
For men to be profited much
By her day upon earth did he sing:
Of her voice, and her steps, and her touch
On the blossoms of tender Spring,
Immortal: and how in her soul
She is with them, and tearless abides,
Folding grain of a love for one goal
In patience, past flowing of tides.
And if unto him she was tears,
He wept not: he wasted within:
Seeming sane in the song, to his peers,
Only crazed where the cravings begin.
Our Lady of Gifts prized he less
Than her issue in darkness: the dim
Lost Skiágeneia's caress
Of our earth made it richest for him.
And for that was a curse on him raised,
And he withered rathe, dry to his prime,
Though the bounteous Giver be praised
Through the island with rites of old time

Exceedingly fervent, and reaped
Veneration for teachings devout,
Pious hymns when the corn-sheaves are heaped,
And the wine-presses ruddily spout,
And the olive and apple are juice
At a touch light as hers lost below.
Whatsoever to men is of use
Sprang his worship of them who bestow,
In a measure of songs unexcelled:
But that soul loving earth and the sun
From her home of the shadows he held
For his beacon where beam there is none:
And to join her, or have her brought back
In his frenzy the singer would call,
Till he followed where never was track,
    On the path trod of all.

THE LARK ASCENDING

He rises and begins to round,
He drops the silver chain of sound,
Of many links without a break,
In chirrup, whistle, slur and shake,
All intervolved and spreading wide,
Like water-dimples down a tide
Where ripple ripple overcurls
And eddy into eddy whirls ;
A press of hurried notes that run
So fleet they scarce are more than one,
Yet changeingly the trills repeat
And linger ringing while they fleet,
Sweet to the quick o' the ear, and dear
To her beyond the handmaid ear,
Who sits beside our inner springs,
Too often dry for this he brings,
Which seems the very jet of earth
At sight of sun, her music's mirth,
As up he wings the spiral stair,
A song of light, and pierces air
With fountain ardour, fountain play,
To reach the shining tops of day,
And drink in everything discerned
An ecstasy to music turned,

Impelled by what his happy bill
Disperses; drinking, showering still,
Unthinking save that he may give
His voice the outlet, there to live
Renewed in endless notes of glee,
So thirsty of his voice is he,
For all to hear and all to know
That he is joy, awake, aglow,
The tumult of the heart to hear
Through pureness filtered crystal-clear,
And know the pleasure sprinkled bright
By simple singing of delight,
Shrill, irreflective, unrestrained,
Rapt, ringing, on the jet sustained
Without a break, without a fall,
Sweet-silvery, sheer lyrical,
Perennial, quavering up the chord
Like myriad dews of sunny sward
That trembling into fulness shine,
And sparkle dropping argentine;
Such wooing as the ear receives
From zephyr caught in choric leaves
Of aspens when their chattering net
Is flushed to white with shivers wet;
And such the water-spirit's chime
On mountain heights in morning's prime,
Too freshly sweet to seem excess,
Too animate to need a stress;
But wider over many heads
The starry voice ascending spreads,
Awakening, as it waxes thin,

The best in us to him akin;
And every face to watch him raised,
Puts on the light of children praised,
So rich our human pleasure ripes
When sweetness on sincereness pipes,
Though nought be promised from the seas,
But only a soft-ruffling breeze
Sweep glittering on a still content,
Serenity in ravishment.

For singing till his heaven fills,
'T is love of earth that he instils,
And ever winging up and up,
Our valley is his golden cup,
And he the wine which overflows
To lift us with him as he goes:
The woods and brooks, the sheep and kine,
He is, the hills, the human line,
The meadows green, the fallows brown,
The dreams of labour in the town;
He sings the sap, the quickened veins;
The wedding song of sun and rains
He is, the dance of children, thanks
Of sowers, shout of primrose-banks,
And eye of violets while they breathe;
All these the circling song will wreathe,
And you shall hear the herb and tree,
The better heart of men shall see,
Shall feel celestially, as long
As you crave nothing save the song.

Was never voice of ours could say
Our inmost in the sweetest way,
Like yonder voice aloft, and link
All hearers in the song they drink.
Our wisdom speaks from failing blood,
Our passion is too full in flood,
We want the key of his wild note
Of truthful in a tuneful throat,
The song seraphically free
Of taint of personality,
So pure that it salutes the suns
The voice of one for millions,
In whom the millions rejoice
For giving their one spirit voice.

Yet men have we, whom we revere,
Now names, and men still housing here,
Whose lives, by many a battle-dint
Defaced, and grinding wheels on flint,
Yield substance, though they sing not, sweet
For song our highest heaven to greet:
Whom heavenly singing gives us new,
Enspheres them brilliant in our blue,
From firmest base to farthest leap,
Because their love of Earth is deep,
And they are warriors in accord
With life to serve, and pass reward,
So touching purest and so heard
In the brain's reflex of yon bird:

Wherefore their soul in me, or mine,
Through self-forgetfulness divine,
In them, that song aloft maintains,
To fill the sky and thrill the plains
With showerings drawn from human stores,
As he to silence nearer soars,
Extends the world at wings and dome,
More spacious making more our home,
Till lost on his aërial rings
In light, and then the fancy sings.

PHOEBUS WITH ADMETUS

I

When by Zeus relenting the mandate was revoked,
  Sentencing to exile the bright Sun-God,
Mindful were the ploughmen of who the steer had yoked,
  Who: and what a track showed the upturned sod!
Mindful were the shepherds as now the noon severe
  Bent a burning eyebrow to brown evetide,
How the rustic flute drew the silver to the sphere,
  Sister of his own, till her rays fell wide.
          God ! of whom music
          And song and blood are pure,
          The day is never darkened
          That had thee here obscure.

II

Chirping none the scarlet cicalas crouched in ranks:
  Slack the thistle-head piled its down-silk grey:
Scarce the stony lizard sucked hollows in his flanks:
  Thick on spots of umbrage our drowsed flocks lay.

Sudden bowed the chestnuts beneath a wind unheard,
    Lengthened ran the grasses, the sky grew slate:
Then amid a swift flight of winged seed white as curd,
    Clear of limb a Youth smote the master's gate.

        God ! of whom music
        And song and blood are pure,
        The day is never darkened
        That had thee here obscure.

III

Water, first of singers, o'er rocky mount and mead,
    First of earthly singers, the sun-loved rill,
Sang of him, and flooded the ripples on the reed,
    Seeking whom to waken and what ear fill.
Water, sweetest soother to kiss a wound and cool,
    Sweetest and divinest, the sky-born brook,
Chuckled, with a whimper, and made a mirror-pool
    Round the guest we welcomed, the strange hand shook.

        God ! of whom music
        And song and blood are pure,
        The day is never darkened
        That had thee here obscure.

IV

Many swarms of wild bees descended on our fields:
    Stately stood the wheatstalk with head bent high:
Big of heart we laboured at storing mighty yields,
    Wool and corn, and clusters to make men cry !

Hand-like rushed the vintage; we strung the bellied skins
  Plump, and at the sealing the Youth's voice rose :
Maidens clung in circle, on little fists their chins;
  Gentle beasties through pushed a cold long nose.
            God! of whom music
            And song and blood are pure,
            The day is never darkened
            That had thee here obscure.

                    V

Foot to fire in snowtime we trimmed the slender shaft :
  Often down the pit spied the lean wolf's teeth
Grin against his will, trapped by masterstrokes of craft;
  Helpless in his froth-wrath as green logs seethe !
Safe the tender lambs tugged the teats, and winter sped
  Whirled before the crocus, the year's new gold.
Hung the hooky beak up aloft the arrowhead
  Reddened through his feathers for our dear fold.
            God! of whom music
            And song and blood are pure,
            The day is never darkened
            That had thee here obscure.

                    VI

Tales we drank of giants at war with Gods above :
  Rocks were they to look on, and earth climbed air !
Tales of search for simples, and those who sought of love
  Ease because the creature was all too fair.

Pleasant ran our thinking that while our work was good,
  Sure as fruits for sweat would the praise come fast.
He that wrestled stoutest and tamed the billow-brood
  Danced in rings with girls, like a sail-flapped mast.
          God! of whom music
          And song and blood are pure,
          The day is never darkened
          That had thee here obscure.

VII

Lo, the herb of healing, when once the herb is known,
  Shines in shady woods bright as new-sprung flame.
Ere the string was tightened we heard the mellow tone,
  After he had taught how the sweet sounds came.
Stretched about his feet, labour done, 't was as you see
  Red pomegranates tumble and burst hard rind.
So began contention to give delight and be
  Excellent in things aimed to make life kind.
          God! of whom music
          And song and blood are pure,
          The day is never darkened
          That had thee here obscure.

VIII

You with shelly horns, rams! and, promontory goats,
  You whose browsing beards dip in coldest dew!
Bulls, that walk the pastures in kingly-flashing coats!
  Laurel, ivy, vine, wreathed for feasts not few!

You that build the shade-roof, and you that court the rays,
  You that leap besprinkling the rock stream-rent:
He has been our fellow, the morning of our days;
  Us he chose for housemates, and this way went.
          God! of whom music
          And song and blood are pure,
          The day is never darkened
          That had thee here obscure.

MELAMPUS

I

With love exceeding a simple love of the things
  That glide in grasses and rubble of woody wreck;
Or change their perch on a beat of quivering wings
  From branch to branch, only restful to pipe and peck;
Or, bristled, curl at a touch their snouts in a ball;
  Or cast their web between bramble and thorny hook;
The good physician Melampus, loving them all,
  Among them walked, as a scholar who reads a book.

II

For him the woods were a home and gave him the key
  Of knowledge, thirst for their treasures in herbs and
      flowers.
The secrets held by the creatures nearer than we
  To earth he sought, and the link of their life with ours:
And where alike we are, unlike where, and the veined
  Division, veined parallel, of a blood that flows
In them, in us, from the source by man unattained
  Save marks he well what the mystical woods disclose.

III

And this he deemed might be boon of love to a breast
　　Embracing tenderly each little motive shape,
The prone, the flitting, who seek their food whither best
　　Their wits direct, whither best from their foes escape:
For closer drawn to our mother's natural milk,
　　As babes they learn where her motherly help is great:
They know the juice for the honey, juice for the silk,
　　And need they medical antidotes find them straight.

IV

Of earth and sun they are wise, they nourish their broods,
　　Weave, build, hive, burrow and battle, take joy and pain
Like swimmers varying billows: never in woods
　　Runs white insanity fleeing itself: all sane
The woods revolve: as the tree its shadowing limns
　　To some resemblance in motion, the rooted life
Restrains disorder: you hear the primitive hymns
　　Of earth in woods issue wild of the web of strife.

V

Now sleeping once on a day of marvellous fire,
　　A brood of snakes he had cherished in grave regret
That death his people had dealt their dam and their sire,
　　Through savage dread of them, crept to his neck, and set
Their tongues to lick him: the swift affectionate tongue
　　Of each ran licking the slumberer: then his ears
A forked red tongue tickled shrewdly: sudden upsprung,
　　He heard a voice piping: Ay, for he has no fears!

VI

A bird said that, in the notes of birds, and the speech
  Of men, it seemed: and another renewed: He moves
To learn and not to pursue, he gathers to teach;
  He feeds his young as do we, and as we love loves.
No fears have I of a man who goes with his head
  To earth, chance looking aloft at us, kind of hand:
I feel to him as to earth of whom we are fed;
  I pipe him much for his good could he understand.

VII

Melampus touched at his ears, laid finger on wrist:
  He was not dreaming, he sensibly felt and heard.
Above, through leaves, where the tree-twigs thick intertwist,
  He spied the birds and the bill of the speaking bird.
His cushion mosses in shades of various green,
  The lumped, the antlered, he pressed, while the sunny
    snake
Slipped under: draughts he had drunk of clear Hippocrene,
  It seemed, and sat with a gift of the Gods awake.

VIII

Divinely thrilled was the man, exultingly full,
  As quick well-waters that come of the heart of earth,
Ere yet they dart in a brook are one bubble-pool
  To light and sound, wedding both at the leap of birth.

The soul of light vivid shone, a stream within stream;
  The soul of sound from a musical shell outflew;
Where others hear but a hum and see but a beam,
  The tongue and eye of the fountain of life he knew.

IX

He knew the Hours: they were round him, laden with seed
  Of hours bestrewn upon vapour, and one by one
They winged as ripened in fruit the burden decreed
  For each to scatter; they flushed like the buds in sun,
Bequeathing seed to successive similar rings,
  Their sisters, bearers to men of what men have earned:
He knew them, talked with the yet unreddened; the
     stings,
  The sweets, they warmed at their bosoms divined,
    discerned.

X

Not unsolicited, sought by diligent feet,
  By riddling fingers expanded, oft watched in growth
With brooding deep as the noon-ray's quickening wheat,
  Ere touch'd, the pendulous flower of the plants of sloth,
The plants of rigidness, answered question and squeeze,
  Revealing wherefore it bloomed uninviting, bent,
Yet making harmony breathe of life and disease,
  The deeper chord of a wonderful instrument.

XI

So passed he luminous-eyed for earth and the fates
   We arm to bruise or caress us: his ears were charged
With tones of love in a whirl of voluble hates,
   With music wrought of distraction his heart enlarged.
Celestial-shining, though mortal, singer, though mute,
   He drew the Master of harmonies, voiced or stilled,
To seek him; heard at the silent medicine-root
   A song, beheld in fulfilment the unfulfilled.

XII

Him Phoebus, lending to darkness colour and form
   Of light's excess, many lessons and counsels gave;
Showed Wisdom lord of the human intricate swarm,
   And whence prophetic it looks on the hives that rave,
And how acquired, of the zeal of love to acquire,
   And where it stands, in the centre of life a sphere;
And Measure, mood of the lyre, the rapturous lyre,
   He said was Wisdom, and struck him the notes to hear.

XIII

Sweet, sweet: 't was glory of vision, honey, the breeze
   In heat, the run of the river on root and stone,
All senses joined, as the sister Pierides
   Are one, uplifting their chorus, the Nine, his own.

In stately order, evolved of sound into sight,
    From sight to sound intershifting, the man descried
The growths of earth, his adored, like day out of night,
    Ascend in song, seeing nature and song allied.

XIV

And there vitality, there, there solely in song,
    Resides, where earth and her uses to men, their needs,
Their forceful cravings, the theme are: there is it strong,
    The Master said: and the studious eye that reads,
(Yea, even as earth to the crown of Gods on the mount),
    In links divine with the lyrical tongue is bound.
Pursue thy craft: it is music drawn of a fount
    To spring perennial; well-spring is common ground.

XV

Melampus dwelt among men: physician and sage,
    He served them, loving them, healing them; sick or
        maimed
Or them that frenzied in some delirious rage
    Outran the measure, his juice of the woods reclaimed.
He played on men, as his master, Phoebus, on strings
    Melodious: as the God did he drive and check,
Through love exceeding a simple love of the things
    That glide in grasses and rubble of woody wreck.

LOVE IN THE VALLEY

UNDER yonder beech-tree single on the green-sward,
  Couched with her arms behind her golden head,
Knees and tresses folded to slip and ripple idly,
  Lies my young love sleeping in the shade.
Had I the heart to slide an arm beneath her,
  Press her parting lips as her waist I gather slow,
Waking in amazement she could not but embrace me :
  Then would she hold me and never let me go ?

.   .   .   .

Shy as the squirrel and wayward as the swallow,
  Swift as the swallow along the river's light
Circleting the surface to meet his mirrored winglets,
  Fleeter she seems in her stay than in her flight.
Shy as the squirrel that leaps among the pine-tops,
  Wayward as the swallow overhead at set of sun,
She whom I love is hard to catch and conquer,
  Hard, but O the glory of the winning were she won !

When her mother tends her before the laughing mirror,
  Tying up her laces, looping up her hair,
Often she thinks, were this wild thing wedded,
  More love should I have, and much less care.

When her mother tends her before the lighted mirror,
  Loosening her laces, combing down her curls,
Often she thinks, were this wild thing wedded,
  I should miss but one for many boys and girls.

.   .   .   .

Heartless she is as the shadow in the meadows
  Flying to the hills on a blue and breezy noon.
No, she is athirst and drinking up her wonder :
  Earth to her is young as the slip of the new moon.
Deals she an unkindness, 't is but her rapid measure,
  Even as in a dance ; and her smile can heal no less :
Like the swinging May-cloud that pelts the flowers with
      hailstones
  Off a sunny border, she was made to bruise and bless.

Lovely are the curves of the white owl sweeping
  Wavy in the dusk lit by one large star.
Lone on the fir-branch, his rattle-note unvaried,
  Brooding o'er the gloom, spins the brown evejar.
Darker grows the valley, more and more forgetting :
  So were it with me if forgetting could be willed.
Tell the grassy hollow that holds the bubbling well-spring,
  Tell it to forget the source that keeps it filled.

.   .   .   .

Stepping down the hill with her fair companions,
  Arm in arm, all against the raying West,
Boldly she sings, to the merry tune she marches,
  Brave is her shape, and sweeter unpossessed.

weeter, for she is what my heart first awaking
  Whispered the world was; morning light is she.
ove that so desires would fain keep her changeless;
  Fain would fling the net, and fain have her free.

appy happy time, when the white star hovers
  Low over dim fields fresh with bloomy dew,
ear the face of dawn, that draws athwart the darkness,
  Threading it with colour, like yewberries the yew.
hicker crowd the shades as the grave East deepens
  Glowing, and with crimson a long cloud swells.
aiden still the morn is; and strange she is, and secret;
  Strange her eyes; her cheeks are cold as cold sea-shells.

  .   .   .   .

nrays, leaning on our southern hills and lighting
  Wild cloud-mountains that drag the hills along,
ft ends the day of your shifting brilliant laughter
  Chill as a dull face frowning on a song.
y, but shows the South-West a ripple-feathered bosom
  Blown to silver while the clouds are shaken and ascend
aling the mid-heavens as they stream, there comes a
        sunset
  Rich, deep like love in beauty without end.

hen at dawn she sighs, and like an infant to the window
  Turns grave eyes craving light, released from dreams,
eautiful she looks, like a white water-lily
  Bursting out of bud in havens of the streams.

When from bed she rises clothed from neck to ankle
    In her long nightgown sweet as boughs of May,
Beautiful she looks, like a tall garden lily
    Pure from the night, and splendid for the day.

.   .   .   .

Mother of the dews, dark eye-lashed twilight,
    Low-lidded twilight, o'er the valley's brim,
Rounding on thy breast sings the dew-delighted skylark,
    Clear as though the dewdrops had their voice in him.
Hidden where the rose-flush drinks the rayless planet,
    Fountain-full he pours the spraying fountain-showers.
Let me hear her laughter, I would have her ever
    Cool as dew in twilight, the lark above the flowers.

All the girls are out with their baskets for the primrose;
    Up lanes, woods through, they troop in joyful bands.
My sweet leads: she knows not why, but now she loiters,
    Eyes the bent anemones, and hangs her hands.
Such a look will tell that the violets are peeping,
    Coming the rose: and unaware a cry
Springs in her bosom for odours and for colour,
    Covert and the nightingale; she knows not why.

.   .   .   .

Kerchiefed head and chin she darts between her tulips,
    Streaming like a willow grey in arrowy rain:
Some bend beaten cheek to gravel, and their angel
    She will be; she lifts them, and on she speeds again.

Black the driving raincloud breasts the iron gateway:
  She is forth to cheer a neighbour lacking mirth.
So when sky and grass met rolling dumb for thunder
  Saw I once a white dove, sole light of earth.

Prim little scholars are the flowers of her garden,
  Trained to stand in rows, and asking if they please.
I might love them well but for loving more the wild ones:
  O my wild ones! they tell me more than these.
You, my wild one, you tell of honied field-rose,
  Violet, blushing eglantine in life; and even as they,
They by the wayside are earnest of your goodness,
  You are of life's, on the banks that line the way.

.   .   .   .

Peering at her chamber the white crowns the red rose,
  Jasmine winds the porch with stars two and three.
Parted is the window; she sleeps; the starry jasmine
  Breathes a falling breath that carries thoughts of me.
Sweeter unpossessed, have I said of her my sweetest?
  Not while she sleeps: while she sleeps the jasmine
      breathes,
Luring her to love; she sleeps; the starry jasmine
  Bears me to her pillow under white rose-wreaths.

Yellow with birdfoot-trefoil are the grass-glades;
  Yellow with cinquefoil of the dew-grey leaf;
Yellow with stonecrop; the moss-mounds are yellow;
  Blue-necked the wheat sways, yellowing to the sheaf.

Green-yellow bursts from the copse the laughing yaffle;
   Sharp as a sickle is the edge of shade and shine:
Earth in her heart laughs looking at the heavens,
   Thinking of the harvest: I look and think of mine.

   .   .   .   .

This I may know: her dressing and undressing
   Such a change of light shows as when the skies in sport
Shift from cloud to moonlight; or edging over thunder
   Slips a ray of sun; or sweeping into port
White sails furl; or on the ocean borders
   White sails lean along the waves leaping green.
Visions of her shower before me, but from eyesight
   Guarded she would be like the sun were she seen.

Front door and back of the mossed old farmhouse
   Open with the morn, and in a breezy link
Freshly sparkles garden to stripe-shadowed orchard,
   Green across a rill where on sand the minnows wink.
Busy in the grass the early sun of summer
   Swarms, and the blackbird's mellow fluting notes
Call my darling up with round and roguish challenge:
   Quaintest, richest carol of all the singing throats!

   .   .   .   .

Cool was the woodside; cool as her white dairy
   Keeping sweet the cream-pan; and there the boys from
      school,
Cricketing below, rushed brown and red with sunshine;
   O the dark translucence of the deep-eyed cool!

Spying from the farm, herself she fetched a pitcher
　　Full of milk, and tilted for each in turn the beak.
Then a little fellow, mouth up and on tiptoe,
　　Said, 'I will kiss you': she laughed and leaned her
　　　　cheek.

Doves of the fir-wood walling high our red roof
　　Through the long noon coo, crooning through the coo.
Loose droop the leaves, and down the sleepy roadway
　　Sometimes pipes a chaffinch; loose droops the blue.
Cows flap a slow tail knee-deep in the river,
　　Breathless, given up to sun and gnat and fly.
Nowhere is she seen; and if I see her nowhere,
　　Lightning may come, straight rains and tiger sky.

.　　.　　.　　.　　.　　.　　.　　.

O the golden sheaf, the rustling treasure-armful!
　　O the nutbrown tresses nodding interlaced!
O the treasure-tresses one another over
　　Nodding! O the girdle slack about the waist!
Slain are the poppies that shot their random scarlet
　　Quick amid the wheatears: wound about the waist,
Gathered, see these brides of Earth one blush of ripeness!
　　O the nutbrown tresses nodding interlaced!

Large and smoky red the sun's cold disk drops,
　　Clipped by naked hills, on violet shaded snow:
Eastward large and still lights up a bower of moonrise,
　　Whence at her leisure steps the moon aglow.

Nightlong on black print-branches our beech-tree
　　Gazes in this whiteness: nightlong could I.
Here may life on death or death on life be painted.
　　Let me clasp her soul to know she cannot die!

．　　　．　　　．　　　．　　　．　　　．

Gossips count her faults; they scour a narrow chamber
　　Where there is no window, read not heaven or her.
'When she was a tiny,' one aged woman quavers,
　　Plucks at my heart and leads me by the ear.
Faults she had once as she learnt to run and tumbled:
　　Faults of feature some see, beauty not complete.
Yet, good gossips, beauty that makes holy
　　Earth and air, may have faults from head to feet.

Hither she comes; she comes to me; she lingers,
　　Deepens her brown eyebrows, while in new surprise
High rise the lashes in wonder of a stranger;
　　Yet am I the light and living of her eyes.
Something friends have told her fills her heart to brimming
　　Nets her in her blushes, and wounds her, and tames. —
Sure of her haven, O like a dove alighting,
　　Arms up, she dropped: our souls were in our names.

．　　　．　　　．　　　．　　　．　　　．

Soon will she lie like a white frost sunrise.
　　Yellow oats and brown wheat, barley pale as rye,
Long since your sheaves have yielded to the thresher,
　　Felt the girdle loosened, seen the tresses fly.

Soon will she lie like a blood-red sunset.
　Swift with the to-morrow, green-winged Spring!
Sing from the South-West, bring her back the truants,
　Nightingale and swallow, song and dipping wing.

Soft new beech-leaves, up to beamy April
　Spreading bough on bough a primrose mountain, you
Lucid in the moon, raise lilies to the skyfields,
　Youngest green transfused in silver shining through:
Fairer than the lily, than the wild white cherry:
　Fair as in image my seraph love appears
Borne to me by dreams when dawn is at my eyelids:
　Fair as in the flesh she swims to me on tears.

.　　.　　.　　.　　.　　.　　.　　.

Could I find a place to be alone with heaven,
　I would speak my heart out: heaven is my need.
Every woodland tree is flushing like the dogwood,
　Flashing like the whitebeam, swaying like the reed.
Flushing like the dogwood crimson in October;
　Streaming like the flag-reed South-West blown;
Flashing as in gusts the sudden-lighted whitebeam:
　All seem to know what is for heaven alone.

THE THREE SINGERS TO YOUNG BLOOD

CAROLS nature, counsel men.
Different notes as rook from wren,
Hear we when our steps begin,
And the choice is cast within,
Where a robber raven's tale
Urges passion's nightingale.

Hark to the three.   Chimed they in one,
Life were music of the sun.
Liquid first, and then the caw,
Then the cry that knows not law.

I

As the birds do, so do we,
Bill our mate, and choose our tree.
Swift to building work addressed,
Any straw will help a nest.
Mates are warm, and this is truth,
Glad the young that come of youth.
They have bloom i' the blood and sap
Chilling at no thunder-clap.
Man and woman on the thorn,
Trust not Earth, and have her scorn.
They who in her lead confide,
Wither me if they spread not wide!
Look for aid to little things,
You will get them quick as wings,
Thick as feathers; would you feed,
Take the leap that springs the need.

II

Contemplate the rutted road :
Life is both a lure and goad.
Each to hold in measure just,
Trample appetite to dust.
Mark the fool and wanton spin :
Keep to harness as a skin.
Ere you follow nature's lead,
Of her powers in you have heed ;
Else a shiverer you will find
You have challenged humankind.
Mates are chosen marketwise :
Coolest bargainer best buys.
Leap not, nor let leap the heart :
Trot your track, and drag your cart.
So your end may be in wool,
Honoured, and with manger full.

III

O the rosy light! it fleets,
Dearer dying than all sweets.
That is life: it waves and goes;
Solely in that cherished Rose
Palpitates, or else 't is death.
Call it love with all thy breath.
Love! it lingers: Love! it nears:
Love! O Love! the Rose appears,
Blushful, magic, reddening air.
Now the choice is on thee: dare!
Mortal seems the touch, but makes
Immortal the hand that takes.
Feel what sea within thee shames
Of its force all other claims,
Drowns them.   Clasp! the world will be
Heavenly Rose to swelling sea.

THE ORCHARD AND THE HEATH

I CHANCED upon an early walk to spy
A troop of children through an orchard gate:
    The boughs hung low, the grass was high;
    They had but to lift hands or wait
For fruits to fill them; fruits were all their sky.

They shouted, running on from tree to tree,
And played the game the wind plays, on and round.
    'T was visible invisible glee
    Pursuing; and a fountain's sound
Of laughter spouted, pattering fresh on me.

I could have watched them till the daylight fled,
Their pretty bower made such a light of day.
    A small one tumbling sang, 'Oh! head!'
    The rest to comfort her straightway
Seized on a branch and thumped down apples red.

The tiny creature flashing through green grass,
And laughing with her feet and eyes among
    Fresh apples, while a little lass
    Over as o'er breeze-ripples hung:
That sight I saw, and passed as aliens pass.

My footpath left the pleasant farms and lanes,
Soft cottage-smoke, straight cocks a-crow, gay flowers ;
    Beyond the wheel-ruts of the wains,
    Across a heath I walked for hours,
And met its rival tenants, rays and rains.

Still in my view mile-distant firs appeared,
When, under a patched channel-bank enriched
    With foxglove whose late bells drooped seared,
    Behold, a family had pitched
Their camp, and labouring the low tent upreared.

Here, too, were many children, quick to scan
A new thing coming ; swarthy cheeks, white teeth :
    In many-coloured rags they ran,
    Like iron runlets of the heath.
Dispersed lay broth-pot, sticks, and drinking-can.

Three girls, with shoulders like a boat at sea
Tipped sideways by the wave (their clothing slid
    From either ridge unequally),
    Lean, swift and voluble, bestrid
A starting-point, unfrocked to the bent knee.

They raced ; their brothers yelled them on, and broke
In act to follow, but as one they snuffed
    Wood-fumes, and by the fire that spoke
    Of provender, its pale flame puffed,
And rolled athwart dwarf furzes grey-blue smoke.

Soon on the dark edge of a ruddier gleam,
The mother-pot perusing, all, stretched flat,
    Paused for its bubbling-up supreme:
    A dog upright in circle sat,
And oft his nose went with the flying steam.

I turned and looked on heaven awhile, where now
The moor-faced sunset broaden'd with red light;
    Threw high aloft a golden bough,
    And seemed the desert of the night
Far down with mellow orchards to endow.

EARTH AND MAN

I

On her great venture, Man,
Earth gazes while her fingers dint the breast
Which is his well of strength, his home of rest,
And fair to scan.

II

More aid than that embrace,
That nourishment, she cannot give: his heart
Involves his fate; and she who urged the start
Abides the race.

III

For he is in the lists
Contentious with the elements, whose dower
First sprang him; for swift vultures to devour
If he desists.

IV

His breath of instant thirst
Is warning of a creature matched with strife,
To meet it as a bride, or let fall life
On life's accursed.

V

No longer forth he bounds
The lusty animal, afield to roam,
But peering in Earth's entrails, where the gnome
Strange themes propounds.

VI

By hunger sharply sped
To grasp at weapons ere he learns their use,
In each new ring he bears a giant's thews,
An infant's head.

VII

And ever that old task
Of reading what he is and whence he came,
Whither to go, finds wilder letters flame
Across her mask.

VIII

She hears his wailful prayer,
When now to the Invisible he raves
To rend him from her, now his mother craves
Her calm, her care.

IX

The thing that shudders most
Within him is the burden of his cry.
Seen of his dread, she is to his blank eye
The eyeless Ghost.

X

Or sometimes she will seem
Heavenly, but her blush, soon wearing white,
Veils like a gorsebush in a web of blight,
With gold-buds dim.

XI

Once worshipped Prime of Powers,
She still was the Implacable : as a beast,
She struck him down and dragged him from the feast
She crowned with flowers.

XII

Her pomp of glorious hues,
Her revelries of ripeness, her kind smile,
Her songs, her peeping faces, lure awhile
With symbol-clues.

XIII

The mystery she holds
For him, inveterately he strains to see,
And sight of his obtuseness is the key
Among those folds.

XIV

He may entreat, aspire,
He may despair, and she has never heed.
She drinking his warm sweat will soothe his need,
Not his desire.

XV

She prompts him to rejoice,
Yet scares him on the threshold with the shroud.
He deems her cherishing of her best-endowed
A wanton's choice.

XVI

Albeit thereof he has found
Firm roadway between lustfulness and pain;
Has half transferred the battle to his brain,
From bloody ground;

XVII

He will not read her good,
Or wise, but with the passion Self obscures;
Through that old devil of the thousand lures,
Through that dense hood:

XVIII

Through terror, through distrust;
The greed to touch, to view, to have, to live:
Through all that makes of him a sensitive
Abhorring dust.

XIX

Behold his wormy home!
And he the wind-whipped, anywhither wave
Crazily tumbled on a shingle-grave
To waste in foam.

XX

Therefore the wretch inclines
Afresh to the Invisible, who, he saith,
Can raise him high : with vows of living faith
For little signs.

XXI

Some signs he must demand,
Some proofs of slaughtered nature ; some prized few,
To satisfy the senses it is true,
And in his hand,

XXII

This miracle which saves
Himself, himself doth from extinction clutch,
By virtue of his worth, contrasting much
With brutes and knaves.

XXIII

From dust, of him abhorred,
He would be snatched by Grace discovering worth.
'Sever me from the hollowness of earth !
Me take, dear Lord ! '

XXIV

She hears him.   Him she owes
For half her loveliness a love well won
By work that lights the shapeless and the dun,
Their common foes.

XXV

He builds the soaring spires,
That sing his soul in stone : of her he draws,
Though blind to her, by spelling at her laws,
Her purest fires.

XXVI

Through him hath she exchanged,
For the gold harvest-robes, the mural crown,
Her haggard quarry-features and thick frown
Where monsters ranged.

XXVII

And order, high discourse,
And decency, than which is life less dear,
She has of him : the lyre of language clear,
Love's tongue and source.

XXVIII

She hears him, and can hear
With glory in his gains by work achieved :
With grief for grief that is the unperceived
In her so near.

XXIX

If he aloft for aid
Imploring storms, her essence is the spur.
His cry to heaven is a cry to her
He would evade.

XXX

Not elsewhere can he tend.
Those are her rules which bid him wash foul sins;
Those her revulsions from the skull that grins
To ape his end.

XXXI

And her desires are those
For happiness, for lastingness, for light.
'T is she who kindles in his haunting night
The hoped dawn-rose.

XXXII

Fair fountains of the dark
Daily she waves him, that his inner dream
May clasp amid the glooms a springing beam,
A quivering lark:

XXXIII

This life and her to know
For Spirit: with awakenedness of glee
To feel stern joy her origin: not he
The child of woe.

XXXIV

But that the senses still
Usurp the station of their issue mind,
He would have burst the chrysalis of the blind:
As yet he will;

XXXV

As yet he will, she prays,
Yet will when his distempered devil of Self ; —
The glutton for her fruits, the wily elf
In shifting rays ; —

XXXVI

That captain of the scorned ;
The coveter of life in soul and shell,
The fratricide, the thief, the infidel,
The hoofed and horned ; —

XXXVII

He singularly doomed
To what he execrates and writhes to shun ; —
When fire has passed him vapour to the sun,
And sun relumed,

XXXVIII

Then shall the horrid pall
Be lifted, and a spirit nigh divine,
'Live in thy offspring as I live in mine,'
Will hear her call.

XXXIX

Whence looks he on a land
Whereon his labour is a carven page;
And forth from heritage to heritage
Nought writ on sand.

XL

His fables of the Above,
And his gapped readings of the crown and sword,
The hell detested and the heaven adored,
The hate, the love,

XLI

The bright wing, the black hoof,
He shall peruse, from Reason not disjoined,
And never unfaith clamouring to be coined
To faith by proof.

XLII

She her just Lord may view,
Not he, her creature, till his soul has yearned
With all her gifts to reach the light discerned
Her spirit through.

XLIII

Then in him time shall run
As in the hour that to young sunlight crows;
And — 'If thou hast good faith it can repose,'
She tells her son.

XLIV

Meanwhile on him, her chief
Expression, her great word of life, looks she;
Twi-minded of him, as the waxing tree,
Or dated leaf.

A BALLAD OF FAIR LADIES IN REVOLT

I

SEE the sweet women, friend, that lean beneath
The ever-falling fountain of green leaves
Round the white bending stem, and like a wreath
Of our most blushful flower shine trembling through,
To teach philosophers the thirst of thieves:
      Is one for me? is one for you?

—Fair sirs, we give you welcome, yield you place,
  And you shall choose among us which you will,
  Without the idle pastime of the chase,
  If to this treaty you can well agree:
  To wed our cause, and its high task fulfil.
      He who's for us, for him are we!

III

- Most gracious ladies, nigh when light has birth,
  A troop of maids, brown as burnt heather-bells,
  And rich with life as moss-roots breathe of earth
  In the first plucking of them, past us flew
  To labour, singing rustic ritornells:
      Had they a cause? are they of you?

IV

— Sirs, they are as unthinking armies are
    To thoughtful leaders, and our cause is theirs.
    When they know men they know the state of war:
    But now they dream like sunlight on a sea,
    And deem you hold the half of happy pairs.
        He who's for us, for him are we!

V

— Ladies, I listened to a ring of dames;
    Judicial in the robe and wig; secure
    As venerated portraits in their frames;
    And they denounced some insurrection new
    Against sound laws which keep you good and pure.
        Are you of them? are they of you?

VI

— Sirs, they are of us, as their dress denotes,
    And by as much: let them together chime:
    It is an ancient bell within their throats,
    Pulled by an aged ringer; with what glee
    Befits the yellow yesterdays of time.
        He who's for us, for him are we!

VII

— Sweet ladies, you with beauty, you with wit;
  Dowered of all favours and all blessed things
  Whereat the ruddy torch of Love is lit;
  Wherefore this vain and outworn strife renew,
  Which stays the tide no more than eddy-rings?
      Who is for love must be for you.

VIII

— The manners of the market, honest sirs,
  'T is hard to quit when you behold the wares.
  You flatter us, or perchance our milliners
  You flatter; so this vain and outworn She
  May still be the charmed snake to your soft airs!
      A higher lord than Love claim we.

IX

 One day, dear lady, missing the broad track,
  I came on a wood's border, by a mead,
  Where golden May ran up to moted black:
  And there I saw Queen Beauty hold review,
  With Love before her throne in act to plead.
      Take him for me, take her for you.

X

— Ingenious gentleman, the tale is known.
Love pleaded sweetly : Beauty would not melt :
She would not melt : he turned in wrath : her throne
The shadow of his back froze witheringly,
And sobbing at his feet Queen Beauty knelt.
    O not such slaves of Love are we !

XI

— Love, lady, like the star above that lance
Of radiance flung by sunset on ridged cloud,
Sad as the last line of a brave romance ! —
Young Love hung dim, yet quivering round him threw
Beams of fresh fire while Beauty waned and bowed.
    Scorn Love, and dread the doom for you.

XII

— Called she not for her mirror, sir ?   Forth ran
Her women : I am lost, she cried, when lo,
Love in the form of an admiring man
Once more in adoration bent the knee
And brought the faded Pagan to full blow :
    For which her throne she gave : not we !

XIII

— My version, madam, runs not to that end.
  A certain madness of an hour half past,
  Caught her like fever : her just lord no friend
  She fancied ; aimed beyond beauty, and thence grew
  The prim acerbity, sweet Love's outcast.
            Great heaven ward off that stroke from you !

XIV

— Your prayer to heaven, good sir, is generous :
  How generous likewise that you do not name
  Offended nature !   She from all of us
  Couched idle underneath our showering tree,
  May quite withhold her most destructive flame ;
            And then what woeful women we !

XV

— Quite, could not be, fair lady ; yet your youth
  May run to drought in visionary schemes :
  And a late waking to perceive the truth,
  When day falls shrouding her supreme adieu,
  Shows darker wastes than unaccomplished dreams :
            And that may be in store for you.

XVI

— O sir, the truth, the truth! is 't in the skies,
Or in the grass, or in this heart of ours?
But O the truth, the truth! the many eyes
That look on it! the diverse things they see,
According to their thirst for fruit or flowers!
      Pass on: it is the truth seek we.

XVII

— Lady, there is a truth of settled laws
That down the past burns like a great watch-fire.
Let youth hail changeful mornings; but your cause,
Whetting its edge to cut the race in two,
Is felony: you forfeit the bright lyre,
      Much honour and much glory you!

XVIII

— Sir, was it glory, was it honour, pride,
And not as cat and serpent and poor slave,
Wherewith we walked in union by your side?
Spare to false womanliness her delicacy,
Or bid true manliness give ear, we crave:
      In our defence thus chained are we.

XIX

— Yours, madam, were the privileges of life
    Proper to man's ideal; you were the mark
    Of action, and the banner in the strife:
    Yea, of your very weakness once you drew
    The strength that sounds the wells, outflies the lark.
        Wrapped in a robe of flame were you!

XX

— Your friend looks thoughtful. Sir, when we were chill,
    You clothed us warmly; all in honour! when
    We starved you fed us ; all in honour still:
    Oh, all in honour, ultra-honourably!
    Deep is the gratitude we owe to men,
        For privileged indeed were we!

XXI

— You cite exceptions, madam, that are sad,
    But come in the red struggle of our growth.
    Alas, that I should have to say it! bad
    Is two-sexed upon earth: this which you do,
    Shows animal impatience, mental sloth:
        Man monstrous, pining seraphs you!

XXII

I fain would ask your friend . . . but I will ask
You, sir, how if in place of numbers vague,
Your sad exceptions were to break that mask
They wear for your cool mind historically,
And blaze like black lists of a *present* plague?
      But in that light behold them we.

XXIII

— Your spirit breathes a mist upon our **world,**
    Lady, and like a rain to pierce the roof
And drench the bed where toil-tossed man lies curled
In his hard-earned oblivion!   You are few,
Scattered, ill-counselled, blinded: for a proof,
      I have lived, and have known none like you.

XXIV

— We may be blind to men, sir: we embrace
    A future now beyond the fowler's nets.
Though few, we hold a promise for the race
That was not at our rising: you are free
To win brave mates; you lose but marionnettes.
      He who's for us, for him are we.

XXV

— Ah! madam, were they puppets who withstood
   Youth's cravings for adventure to preserve
   The dedicated ways of womanhood?
   The light which leads us from the paths of rue,
   That light above us, never seen to swerve,
      Should be the home-lamp trimmed by you.

XXVI

— Ah! sir, our worshipped posture we perchance
   Shall not abandon, though we see not how,
   Being to that lamp-post fixed, we may advance
   Beside our lords in any real degree,
   Unless we move: and to advance is now
      A sovereign need, think more than we.

XXVII

— So push you out of harbour in small craft,
   With little seamanship; and comes a gale,
   The world will laugh, the world has often laughed,
   Lady, to see how bold when skies are blue,
   When black winds churn the deeps how panic-pale,
      How swift to the old nest fly you!

XXVIII

–What thinks your friend, kind sir ?   We have escaped
But partly that old half-tamed wild beast's paw
Whereunder woman, the weak thing, was shaped:
Men too have known the cramping enemy
In grim brute force, whom force of brain shall awe:
      Him our deliverer, await we !

XXIX

– Delusions are with eloquence endowed,
And yours might pluck an angel from the spheres
To play in this revolt whereto you are vowed,
Deliverer, lady ! but like summer dew
O'er fields that crack for rain your friends drop tears,
      Who see the awakening for you.

XXX

–Is he our friend, there silent ? he weeps not.
O sir, delusion mounting like a sun
On a mind blank as the white wife of Lot,
Giving it warmth and movement! if this be
Delusion, think of what thereby was won
      For men, and dream of what win we.

XXXI

—Lady, the destiny of minor powers,
    Who would recast us, is but to convulse:
You enter on a strife that frets and sours;
You can but win sick disappointment's hue;
And simply an accelerated pulse,
        Some tonic you have drunk moves you.

XXXII

—Thinks your friend so? Good sir, your wit is bright;
    But wit that strives to speak the popular voice,
Puts on its nightcap and puts out its light;
Curfew, would seem your conqueror's decree
To women likewise: and we have no choice
        Save darkness or rebellion, we!

XXXIII

—A plain safe intermediate way is cleft
    By reason foiling passion: you that rave
Of mad alternatives to right and left
Echo the tempter, madam: and 't is due
Unto your sex to shun it as the grave,
        This later apple offered you.

XXXIV

— This apple is not ripe, it is not sweet;
  Nor rosy, sir, nor golden : eye and mouth
Are little wooed by it; yet we would eat.
We are somewhat tired of Eden, is our plea.
We have thirsted long; this apple suits our drouth :
      'T is good for men to halve, think we.

XXXV

— But say, what seek you, madam ?   'T is enough
That you should have dominion o'er the springs
Domestic and man's heart : those ways, how rough,
How vile, outside the stately avenue
Where you walk sheltered by your angel's wings,
      Are happily unknown to you.

XXXVI

— We hear women's shrieks on them.   We like your phrase,
Dominion domestic !   And that roar,
'What seek you ?' is of tyrants in all days.
Sir, get you something of our purity,
And we will of your strength : we ask no more.
      That is the sum of what seek we.

XXXVII

— O for an image, madam, in one word,
  To show you as the lightning night reveals,
  Your error and your perils : you have erred
  In mind only, and the perils that ensue
  Swift heels may soften ; wherefore to swift heels
      Address your hopes of safety you !

XXXVIII

— To err in mind, sir . . . your friend smiles : he may !
  To err in mind, if err in mind we can,
  Is grievous error you do well to stay.
  But O how different from reality
  Men's fiction is ! how like you in the plan,
      Is woman, knew you her as we !

XXXIX

— Look, lady, where yon river winds its line
  Toward sunset, and receives on breast and face
  The splendour of fair life : to be divine,
  'T is nature bids you be to nature true,
  Flowing with beauty, lending earth your grace,
      Reflecting heaven in clearness you.

XL

— Sir, you speak well: your friend no word vouchsafes.
To flow with beauty, breeding fools and worse,
Cowards and worse: at such fair life she chafes
Who is not wholly of the nursery,
Nor of your schools: we share the primal curse;
      Together shake it off, say we!

XLI

— Here, then, my friend, madam!   Tongue-restrained he
    stands
Till words are thoughts, and thoughts, like swords
    enriched
With traceries of the artificer's hands,
Are fire-proved steel to cut, fair flowers to view. —
Do I hear him?   Oh, he is bewitched, bewitched!
      Heed him not!   Traitress beauties you!

XLII

— We have won a champion, sisters, and a sage!
— Ladies, you win a guest to a good feast!
— Sir spokesman, sneers are weakness veiling rage.
— Of weakness, and wise men, you have the key.
— Then are there fresher mornings mounting East
      Than ever yet have dawned, sing we!

XLIII

- False ends as false began, madam, be sure!
- What lure there is the pure cause purifies!
- Who purifies the victim of the lure?
— That soul which bids us our high light pursue.
— Some heights are measured down: the wary wise
       Shun Reason in the masque with you!

XLIV

— Sir, for the friend you bring us, take our thanks
  Yes, Beauty was of old this barren goal;
  A thing with claws; and brute-like in her pranks!
  But could she give more loyal guarantee
  Than wooing wisdom, that in her a soul
      Has risen?   Adieu: content are we!

XLV

Those ladies led their captive to the flood's
  Green edge.   He floating with them seemed the most
Fool-flushed old noddy ever crowned with buds.
Happier than I!   Then, why not wiser too?
For he that lives with Beauty, he may boast
      His comrade over me and you.

XLVI

Have women nursed some dream since Helen sailed
Over the sea of blood the blushing star,
That beauty, whom frail man as Goddess hailed,
When not possessing her (for such is he!),
Might in a wondering season seen afar,
      Be tamed to say not 'I,' but 'we'?

XLVII

And shall they make of Beauty their estate,
The fortress and the weapon of their sex?
Shall she in her frost-brilliancy dictate,
More queenly than of old, how we must woo,
Ere she will melt?   The halter's on our necks,
      Kick as it likes us, I and you.

XLVIII

Certain it is, if Beauty has disdained
Her ancient conquests, with an aim thus high:
If this, if that, if more, the fight is gained.
But can she keep her followers without fee?
Yet ah! to hear anew those ladies cry,
      He who's for us, for him are we!

JUGGLING JERRY

I

PITCH here the tent, while the old horse grazes·
    By the old hedge-side we 'll halt a stage.
It 's nigh my last above the daisies:
    My next leaf 'll be man's blank page.
Yes, my old girl! and it 's no use crying:
    Juggler, constable, king, must bow.
One that outjuggles all 's been spying
    Long to have me, and he has me now.

II

We 've travelled times to this old common:
    Often we 've hung our pots in the gorse.
We 've had a stirring life, old woman!
    You, and I, and the old grey horse.
Races, and fairs, and royal occasions,
    Found us coming to their call:
Now they 'll miss us at our stations:
    There 's a Juggler outjuggles all!

III

Up goes the lark, as if all were jolly!
  Over the duck-pond the willow shakes.
Easy to think that grieving 's folly,
  When the hand 's firm as driven stakes!
Ay, when we 're strong, and braced, and manful,
  Life 's a sweet fiddle: but we 're a batch
Born to become the Great Juggler's han'ful:
  Balls he shies up, and is safe to catch.

IV

Here 's where the lads of the village cricket:
  I was a lad not wide from here:
Could n't I whip off the bale from the wicket?
  Like an old world those days appear!
Donkey, sheep, geese, and thatched ale-house — I know
    them!
  They are old friends of my halts, and seem,
Somehow, as if kind thanks I owe them:
  Juggling don't hinder the heart's esteem.

V

Juggling 's no sin, for we must have victual:
  Nature allows us to bait for the fool.
Holding one's own makes us juggle no little;
  But, to increase it, hard juggling 's the rule.
You that are sneering at my profession,
  Have n't you juggled a vast amount?
There 's the Prime Minister, in one Session,
  Juggles more games than my sins 'll count.

VI

I 've murdered insects with mock thunder:
    Conscience, for that, in men don't quail.
I 've made bread from the bump of wonder:
    That 's my business, and there 's my tale.
Fashion and rank all praised the professor:
    Ay! and I 've had my smile from the Queen:
Bravo, Jerry! she meant: God bless her!
    Ain't this a sermon on that scene?

VII

I 've studied men from my topsy-turvy
    Close, and, I reckon, rather true.
Some are fine fellows: some, right scurvy:
    Most, a dash between the two.
But it 's a woman, old girl, that makes me
    Think more kindly of the race:
And it 's a woman, old girl, that shakes me
    When the Great Juggler I must face.

VIII

We two were married, due and legal:
    Honest we 've lived since we 've been one.
Lord! I could then jump like an eagle:
    You danced bright as a bit o' the sun.
Birds in a May-bush we were! right merry!
    All night we kiss'd, we juggled all day.
Joy was the heart of Juggling Jerry!
    Now from his old girl he 's juggled away.

IX

It 's past parsons to console us:
    No, nor no doctor fetch for me:
I can die without my bolus;
    Two of a trade, lass, never agree!
Parson and Doctor! — don't they love rarely,
    Fighting the devil in other men's fields!
Stand up yourself and match him fairly:
    Then see how the rascal yields !

X

I, lass, have lived no gipsy, flaunting
    Finery while his poor helpmate grubs:
Coin I 've stored, and you won't be wanting:
    You sha'n't beg from the troughs and tubs.
Nobly you 've stuck to me, though in his kitchen
    Many a Marquis would hail you Cook !
Palaces you could have ruled and grown rich in,
    But your old Jerry you never forsook.

XI

Hand up the chirper! ripe ale winks in it;
    Let 's have comfort and be at peace.
Once a stout draught made me light as a linnet.
· Cheer up! the Lord must have his lease.
May be — for none see in that black hollow —
    It 's just a place where we 're held in pawn,
And, when the Great Juggler makes as to swallow,
    It 's just the sword-trick — I ain't quite gone!

XII

Yonder came smells of the gorse, so nutty,
    Gold-like and warm: it's the prime of May.
Better than mortar, brick and putty,
    Is God's house on a blowing day.
Lean me more up the mound; now I feel it:
    All the old heath-smells!   Ain't it strange?
There's the world laughing, as if to conceal it,
    But He's by us, juggling the change.

XIII

I mind it well, by the sea-beach lying,
    Once — it's long gone — when two gulls we beheld,
Which, as the moon got up, were flying
    Down a big wave that sparked and swelled.
Crack, went a gun: one fell: the second
    Wheeled round him twice, and was off for new luck:
There in the dark her white wing beckon'd: —
    Drop me a kiss — I'm the bird dead-struck!

THE OLD CHARTIST

I

WHATE'ER I be, old England is my dam!
  So there's my answer to the judges, clear.
I'm nothing of a fox, nor of a lamb;
  I don't know how to bleat nor how to leer:
        I'm for the nation!
  That's why you see me by the wayside here,
    Returning home from transportation.

II

It's Summer in her bath this morn, I think
  I'm fresh as dew, and chirpy as the birds.
And just for joy to see old England wink
  Thro' leaves again, I could harangue the herds:
        Is n't it something
  To speak out like a man when you've got words,
    And prove you're not a stupid dumb thing?

III

They shipp'd me off for it; I'm here again.
  Old England is my dam, whate'er I be!
Says I, I'll tramp it home, and see the grain:
    If you see well, you're king of what you see:
          Eyesight is having,
    If you're not given, I said, to gluttony.
      Such talk to ignorance sounds as raving.

IV

You dear old brook, that from his Grace's park
  Come bounding! on you run near my old town:
My lord can't lock the water; nor the lark,
    Unless he kills him, can my lord keep down.
          Up, is the song-note!
    I've tried it, too:—for comfort and renown,
      I rather pitch'd upon the wrong note.

V

I'm not ashamed: Not beaten's still my boast:
  Again I'll rouse the people up to strike.
But home's where different politics jar most.
    Respectability the women like.
          This form, or that form,—
    The Government may be hungry pike,
      But don't you mount a Chartist platform!

VI

Well, well! Not beaten — spite of them, I shout;
    And my estate is suffering for the Cause. —
No, — what is yon brown water-rat about,
    Who washes his old poll with busy paws?
             What does he mean by 't?
It 's like defying all our natural laws,
    For him to hope that he 'll get clean by 't.

VII

His seat is on a mud-bank, and his trade
    Is dirt: — he 's quite contemptible; and yet
The fellow 's all as anxious as a maid
    To show a decent dress, and dry the wet.
             Now it 's his whisker,
And now his nose, and ear: he seems to get
    Each moment at the motion brisker!

VIII

To see him squat like little chaps at school,
    I could let fly a laugh with all my might.
He peers, hangs both his fore-paws: — bless that fool,
    He 's bobbing at his frill now! — what a sight!
             Licking the dish up,
As if he thought to pass from black to white,
    Like parson into lawny bishop.

IX

The elms and yellow reed-flags in the sun,
  Look on quite grave : — the sunlight flecks his side;
And links of bindweed-flowers round him run,
  And shine up doubled with him in the tide.
      I 'm nearly splitting,
  But nature seems like seconding his pride,
    And thinks that his behaviour 's fitting.

X

That isle o' mud looks baking dry with gold.
  His needle-muzzle still works out and in.
It really is a wonder to behold,
  And makes me feel the bristles of my chin.
      Judged by appearance,
  I fancy of the two I 'm nearer Sin,
    And might as well commence a clearance.

XI

And that 's what my fine daughter said : — she meant :
  Pray, hold your tongue, and wear a Sunday face.
Her husband, the young linendraper, spent
  Much argument thereon : — I 'm their disgrace.
      Bother the couple !
  I feel superior to a chap whose place
    Commands him to be neat and supple.

XII

But if I go and say to my old hen:
   I 'll mend the gentry's boots, and keep discreet,
Until they grow *too* violent, — why, then,
   A warmer welcome I might chance to meet:
         Warmer and better.
   And if she fancies her old cock is beat,
     And drops upon her knees — so let her !

XIII

She suffered for me: — women, you 'll observe,
   Don't suffer for a Cause, but for a man.
When I was in the dock she show'd her nerve:
   I saw beneath her shawl my old tea-can.
        Trembling . . . she brought it
   To screw me for my work: she loath'd my plan,
     And therefore doubly kind I thought it.

XIV

I 've never lost the taste of that same tea:
   That liquor on my logic floats like oil,
When I state facts, and fellows disagree.
   For human creatures all are in a coil;
        All may want pardon.
   I see a day when every pot will boil
     Harmonious in one great Tea-garden !

XV

We wait the setting of the Dandy's day,
　　Before that time! — He's furbishing his dress, -
He *will* be ready for it! — and I say,
　　That yon old dandy rat amid the cress, —
　　　　Thanks to hard labour! —
　　If cleanliness is next to godliness,
　　　　The old fat fellow's heaven's neighbour!

XVI

You teach me a fine lesson, my old boy!
　　I've looked on my superiors far too long,
And small has been my profit as my joy.
　　You've done the right while I've denounced the wrong.
　　　　Prosper me later!
　　Like you I will despise the sniggering throng,
　　　　And please myself and my Creator.

XVII

I'll bring the linendraper and his wife
　　Some day to see you ; taking off my hat.
Should they ask why, I'll answer: in my life
　　I never found so true a democrat.
　　　　Base occupation
　　Can't rob you of your own esteem, old rat!
　　　　I'll preach you to the British nation.

MARTIN'S PUZZLE

I

THERE she goes up the street with her book in her hand,
  And her Good morning, Martin! Ay, lass, how d'ye do?
Very well, thank you, Martin! — I can't understand!
  I might just as well never have cobbled a shoe!
I can't understand it.   She talks like a song;
  Her voice takes your ear like the ring of a glass;
She seems to give gladness while limping along,
  Yet sinner ne'er suffer'd like that little lass.

II

First, a fool of a boy ran her down with a cart.
  Then, her fool of a father — a blacksmith by trade —
Why the deuce does he tell us it half broke his heart?
  His heart! — where's the leg of the poor little maid!
Well, that's not enough; they must push her downstairs,
  To make her go crooked: but why count the list?
If it's right to suppose that our human affairs
  Are all order'd by heaven — there, bang goes my fist!

III

For if angels can look on such sights — never mind!
 When you 're next to blaspheming, it 's best to be mum,
The parson declares that her woes were n't designed;
 But, then, with the parson it 's all kingdom-come.
Lose a leg, save a soul — a convenient text;
 I call it Tea doctrine, not savouring of God.
When poor little Molly wants 'chastening,' why, next
 The Archangel Michael might taste of the rod.

IV

But, to see the poor darling go limping for miles
 To read books to sick people! — and just of an age
When girls learn the meaning of ribands and smiles!
 Makes me feel like a squirrel that turns in a cage.
The more I push thinking the more I revolve:
 I never get farther: — and as to her face,
It starts up when near on my puzzle I solve,
 And says, 'This crush'd body seems such a sad case.'

V

Not that she 's for complaining: she reads to earn pence;
 And from those who can't pay, simple thanks are enough.
Does she leave lamentation for chaps without sense?
 Howsoever, she 's made up of wonderful stuff.
Ay, the soul in her body must be a stout cord;
 She sings little hymns at the close of the day,
Though she has but three fingers to lift to the Lord,
 And only one leg to kneel down with to pray.

VI

What I ask is, Why persecute such a poor dear,
    If there 's Law above all ?   Answer that if you can !
Irreligious I 'm not; but I look on this sphere
    As a place where a man should just think like a man.
It is n't fair dealing! But, contrariwise,
    Do bullets in battle the wicked select ?
Why, then it 's all chance-work ! And yet, in her eyes,
    She holds a fixed something by which I am checked.

VII

Yonder riband of sunshine aslope on the wall,
    If you eye it a minute 'll have the same look :
So kind! and so merciful ! God of us all !
    It 's the very same lesson we get from the Book.
Then, is Life but a trial ? Is that what is meant ?
    Some must toil, and some perish, for others below:
The injustice to each spreads a common content;
    Ay ! I 've lost it again, for it can't be quite so.

VIII

She 's the victim of fools : that seems nearer the mark.
    On earth there are engines and numerous fools.
Why the Lord can permit them, we 're still in the dark;
    He does, and in some sort of way they 're his tools.
It 's a roundabout way, with respect let me add,
    If Molly goes crippled that we may be taught :
But, perhaps, it 's the only way, though it 's so bad;
    In that case we 'll bow down our heads, — as we ought.

IX

But the worst of *me* is, that when I bow my head,
　I perceive a thought wriggling away in the dust,
And I follow its tracks, quite forgetful, instead
　Of humble acceptance : for, question I must!
Here 's a creature made carefully — carefully made !
　Put together with craft, and then stamped on, and why ?
The answer seems nowhere : it 's discord that 's played.
　The sky 's a blue dish !— an implacable sky !

X

Stop a moment.　I seize an idea from the pit.
　They tell us that discord, though discord, alone,
Can be harmony when the notes properly fit :
　Am I judging all things from a single false tone ?
Is the Universe one immense Organ, that rolls
　From devils to angels ?　I 'm blind with the sight.
It pours such a splendour on heaps of poor souls !
　I might try at kneeling with Molly to-night.

MARIAN

SHE can be as wise as we,
    And wiser when she wishes;
She can knit with cunning wit,
    And dress the homely dishes.
She can flourish staff or pen,
    And deal a wound that lingers;
She can talk the talk of men,
    And touch with thrilling fingers.

II

Match her ye across the sea,
    Natures fond and fiery;
Ye who zest the turtle's nest
    With the eagle's eyrie.
Soft and loving is her soul,
    Swift and lofty soaring;
Mixing with its dove-like dole
    Passionate adoring.

III

Such a she who 'll match with **me**?
　　In flying or pursuing,
Subtle wiles are in her smiles
　　To set the world a-wooing.
She is steadfast as a star,
　　And yet the maddest maiden:
She can wage a gallant war,
　　And give the peace of **Eden**.

SONNETS

LUCIFER IN STARLIGHT

On a starred night Prince Lucifer uprose.
Tired of his dark dominion swung the fiend
Above the rolling ball in cloud part screened,
Where sinners hugged their spectre of repose.
Poor prey to his hot fit of pride were those.
And now upon his western wing he leaned,
Now his huge bulk o'er Afric's sands careened,
Now the black planet shadowed Arctic snows.
Soaring through wider zones that pricked his scars
With memory of the old revolt from Awe,
He reached a middle height, and at the stars,
Which are the brain of heaven, he looked, and sank.
Around the ancient track marched rank on rank,
The army of unalterable law.

THE STAR SIRIUS

Bright Sirius ! that when Orion pales
To dotlings under moonlight still art keen
With cheerful fervour of a warrior's mien
Who holds in his great heart the battle-scales :
Unquenched of flame though swift the flood assails,
Reducing many lustrous to the lean :
Be thou my star, and thou in me be seen
To show what source divine is, and prevails.
Long watches through, at one with godly night,
I mark thee planting joy in constant fire ;
And thy quick beams, whose jets of life inspire
Life to the spirit, passion for the light,
Dark Earth since first she lost her lord from sight
Has viewed and felt them sweep her as a lyre.

SENSE AND SPIRIT

THE senses loving Earth or well or ill,
Ravel yet more the riddle of our lot.
The mind is in their trammels, and lights not
By trimming fear-bred tales; nor does the will
To find in nature things which less may chill
An ardour that desires, unknowing what.
Till we conceive her living we go distraught,
At best but circle-windsails of a mill.
Seeing she lives, and of her joy of life
Creatively has given us blood and breath
For endless war and never wound unhealed,
The gloomy Wherefore of our battle-field
Solves in the Spirit, wrought of her through strife
To read her own and trust her down to death.

EARTH'S SECRET

NOT solitarily in fields we find
Earth's secret open, though one page is there;
Her plainest, such as children spell, and share
With bird and beast; raised letters for the blind.
Not where the troubled passions toss the mind,
In turbid cities, can the key be bare.
It hangs for those who hither thither fare,
Close interthreading nature with our kind.
They, hearing History speak, of what men were,
And have become, are wise.   The gain is great
In vision and solidity; it lives.
Yet at a thought of life apart from her,
Solidity and vision lose their state,
For Earth, that gives the milk, the spirit gives.

THE SPIRIT OF SHAKESPEARE

THY greatest knew thee, Mother Earth; unsoured
He knew thy sons.   He probed from hell to hell
Of human passions, but of love deflowered
His wisdom was not, for he knew thee well.
Thence came the honeyed corner at his lips,
The conquering smile wherein his spirit sails
Calm as the God who the white sea-wave whips,
Yet full of speech and intershifting tales,
Close mirrors of us : thence had he the laugh
We feel is thine : broad as ten thousand beeves
At pasture ! thence thy songs, that winnow chaff
From grain, bid sick Philosophy's last leaves
Whirl, if they have no response — they enforced
To fatten Earth when from her soul divorced.

THE SPIRIT OF SHAKESPEARE (*continued*)

How smiles he at a generation ranked
In gloomy noddings over life !   They pass.
Not he to feed upon a breast unthanked,
Or eye a beauteous face in a cracked glass.
But he can spy that little twist of brain
Which moved some weighty leader of the blind,
Unwitting 't was the goad of personal pain,
To view in curst eclipse our Mother's mind,
And show us of some rigid harridan
The wretched bondmen till the end of time.
O lived the Master now to paint us Man,
That little twist of brain would ring a chime
Of whence it came and what it caused, to start
Thunders of laughter, clearing air and heart.

INTERNAL HARMONY

Assured of worthiness we do not dread
Competitors; we rather give them hail
And greeting in the lists where we may fail:
Must, if we bear an aim beyond the head!
My betters are my masters: purely fed
By their sustainment I likewise shall scale
Some rocky steps between the mount and vale;
Meanwhile the mark I have and I will wed.
So that I draw the breath of finer air,
Station is nought, nor footways laurel-strewn,
Nor rivals tightly belted for the race.
Good speed to them! My place is here or there;
My pride is that among them I have place:
And thus I keep this instrument in tune.

GRACE AND LOVE

Two flower-enfolding crystal vases she
I love fills daily, mindful but of one:
And close behind pale morn she, like the sun
Priming our world with light, pours, sweet to see,
Clear water in the cup, and into me
The image of herself: and that being done,
Choice of what blooms round her fair garden run
In climbers or in creepers or the tree,
She ranges with unerring fingers fine,
To harmony so vivid that through sight
I hear, I have her heavenliness to fold
Beyond the senses, where such love as mine,
Such grace as hers, should the strange Fates withhold
Their starry more from her and me, unite.

APPRECIATION

EARTH was not Earth before her sons appeared,
Nor Beauty Beauty ere young Love was born:
And thou when I lay hidden wast as morn
At city-windows, touching eyelids bleared;
To none by her fresh wingedness endeared;
Unwelcome unto revellers outworn.
I the last echoes of Diana's horn
In woodland heard, and saw thee come, and cheered.
No longer wast thou then mere light, fair soul!
And more than simple duty moved thy feet.
New colours rose in thee, from fear, from shame,
From hope, effused: though not less pure a scroll
May men read on the heart I taught to beat:
That change in thee, if not thyself, I claim.

THE DISCIPLINE OF WISDOM

Rich labour is the struggle to be wise,
While we make sure the struggle cannot cease.
Else better were it in some bower of peace
Slothful to swing, contending with the flies.
You point at Wisdom fixed on lofty skies,
As mid barbarian hordes a sculptured Greece:
She falls.   To live and shine, she grows her fleece,
Is shorn, and rubs with follies and with lies.
So following her, your hewing may attain
The right to speak unto the mute, and shun
That sly temptation of the illumined brain,
Deliveries oracular, self-spun.
Who sweats not with the flock will seek in vain
To shed the words which are ripe fruit of sun.

THE STATE OF AGE

RUB thou thy battered lamp: nor claim nor beg
Honours from aught about thee.   Light the young.
Thy frame is as a dusty mantle hung,
O grey one! pendant on a loosened peg.
Thou art for this our life an ancient egg,
Or a tough bird: thou hast a rudderless tongue,
Turning dead trifles, like the cock of dung;
Which runs, Time's contrast to thy halting leg.
Nature, it is most sure, not thee admires.
But hast thou in thy season set her fires
To burn from Self to Spirit through the lash,
Honoured the sons of Earth shall hold thee high:
Yea, to spread light when thy proud letter I
Drops prone and void as any thoughtless dash.

PROGRESS

In Progress you have little faith, say you:
Men will maintain dear interests, wreak base hates,
By force, and gentle women choose their mates
Most amorously from the gilded fighting crew:
The human heart Bellona's mad halloo
Will ever fire to dicing with the Fates.
'Now at this time,' says History, 'those two States
'Stood ready their past wrestling to renew.
'They sharpened arms and showed them, like the brutes
'Whose haunches quiver. But a yellow blight
'Fell on their waxing harvests. They deferred
'The bloody settlement of their disputes
'Till God should bless them better.' They did right.
And naming Progress, both shall have the word.

THE WORLD'S ADVANCE

Judge mildly the tasked world; and disincline
To brand it, for it bears a heavy pack.
You have perchance observed the inebriate's track
At night when he has quitted the inn-sign:
He plays diversions on the homeward line,
Still that way bent albeit his legs are slack:
A hedge may take him, but he turns not back,
Nor turns this burdened world, of curving spine.
'Spiral,' the memorable Lady terms
Our mind's ascent: our world's advance presents
That figure on a flat; the way of worms.
Cherish the promise of its good intents,
And warn it, not one instinct to efface
Ere Reason ripens for the vacant place.

A CERTAIN PEOPLE

As Puritans they prominently wax,
And none more kindly gives and takes hard knocks.
Strong psalmic chanting, like to nasal cocks,
They join to thunderings of their hearty thwacks.
But naughtiness, with hoggery, not lacks
When Peace another door in them unlocks,
Where conscience shows the eyeing of an ox
Grown dully apprehensive of an Axe.
Graceless they are when gone to frivolousness,
Fearing the God they flout, the God they glut.
They need their pious exercises less
Than schooling in the Pleasures: fair belief
That these are devilish only to their thief,
Charged with an Axe nigh on the occiput

THE GARDEN OF EPICURUS

THAT Garden of sedate Philosophy
Once flourished, fenced from passion and mishap,
A shining spot upon a shaggy map;
Where mind and body, in fair junction free,
Luted their joyful concord; like the tree
From root to flowering twigs a flowing sap.
Clear Wisdom found in tended Nature's lap,
Of gentlemen the happy nursery.
That Garden would on light supremest verge,
Were the long drawing of an equal breath
Healthful for Wisdom's head, her heart, her aims.
Our world which for its Babels wants a scourge,
And for its wilds a husbandman, acclaims
The crucifix that came of Nazareth.

A LATER ALEXANDRIAN

An inspiration caught from dubious hues,
Filled him, and mystic wrynesses he chased;
For they lead farther than the single-faced,
Wave subtler promise when desire pursues.
The moon of cloud discoloured was his Muse,
His pipe the reed of the old moaning waste.
Love was to him with anguish fast enlaced,
And Beauty where she walked blood-shot the dews.
Men railed at such a singer; women thrilled
Responsively: he sang not Nature's own
Divinest, but his lyric had a tone,
As 't were a forest-echo of her voice:
What barrenly they yearn for seemed distilled
From what they dread, who do through tears rejoice.

AN ORSON OF THE MUSE

Her son, albeit the Muse's livery
And measured courtly paces rouse his taunts,
Naked and hairy in his savage haunts,
To Nature only will he bend the knee;
Spouting the founts of her distillery
Like rough rock-sources; and his woes and wants,
Being Nature's, civil limitation daunts
His utterance never; the nymphs blush, not he.
Him, when he blows of Earth, and Man, and Fate,
The Muse will hearken to with graver ear
Than many of her train can waken: him
Would fain have taught what fruitful things and dear
Must sink beneath the tidewaves, of their weight,
If in no vessel built for sea they swim.

THE POINT OF TASTE

UNHAPPY poets of a sunken prime!
You to reviewers are as ball to bat.
They shadow you with Homer, knock you flat
With Shakespeare: bludgeons brainingly sublime
On you the excommunicates of Rhyme,
Because you sing not in the living Fat.
The wiry whizz of an intrusive gnat
Is verse that shuns their self-producing time.
Sound them their clocks, with loud alarum trump,
Or watches ticking temporal at their fobs,
You win their pleased attention. But, bright God
O' the lyre, what bully-drawlers they applaud!
Rather for us a tavern-catch, and bump
Chorus where Lumpkin with his Giles hobnobs.

CAMELUS SALTAT

What say you, critic, now you have become
An author and maternal ? — in this trap
(To quote you) of poor hollow folk who rap
On instruments as like as drum to drum.
You snarled tut-tut for welcome to tum-tum,
So like the nose fly-teased in its noon's nap.
You scratched an insect-slaughtering thunder-clap
With that between the fingers and the thumb.
It seemeth mad to quit the Olympian couch,
Which bade our public gobble or reject.
O spectacle of Peter, shrewdly pecked,
Piper, by his own pepper from his pouch!
What of the sneer, the jeer, the voice austere,
You dealt ? — the voice austere, the jeer, the sneer.

CAMELUS SALTAT (*continued*)

ORACLE of the market! thence you drew
The taste which stamped you guide of the inept. —
A North-sea pilot, Hildebrand yclept,
A sturdy and a briny, once men knew.
He loved small beer, and for that copious brew,
To roll ingurgitation till he slept,
Rations exchanged with flavour for the adept:
And merrily plied him captain, mate and crew.
At last this dancer to the Polar star
Sank, washed out within, and overboard was pitched,
To drink the sea and pilot him to land.
O captain-critic! printed, neatly stitched,
Know, while the pillory-eggs fly fast, they are
Not eggs, but the drowned soul of Hildebrand.

TO J. M.

Let Fate or Insufficiency provide
Mean ends for men who what they are would be:
Penned in their narrow day no change they see
Save one which strikes the blow to brutes and pride.
Our faith is ours and comes not on a tide:
And whether Earth's great offspring, by decree,
Must rot if they abjure rapacity,
Not argument but effort shall decide.
They number many heads in that hard flock:
Trim swordsmen they push forth: yet try thy steel.
Thou, fighting for poor humankind, wilt feel
The strength of Roland in thy wrist to hew
A chasm sheer into the barrier rock,
And bring the army of the faithful through.

TO A FRIEND LOST

(T. T.)

WHEN I remember, friend, whom lost I call,
Because a man beloved is taken hence,
The tender humour and the fire of sense
In your good eyes; how full of heart for all,
And chiefly for the weaker by the wall,
You bore that lamp of sane benevolence;
Then see I round you Death his shadows dense
Divide, and at your feet his emblems fall.
For surely are you one with the white host,
Spirits, whose memory is our vital air
Through the great love of Earth they had: lo, these,
Like beams that throw the path on tossing seas,
Can bid us feel we keep them in the ghost,
Partakers of a strife they joyed to share.

MY THEME

Of me and of my theme think what thou wilt:
The song of gladness one straight bolt can check.
But I have never stood at Fortune's beck:
Were she and her light crew to run atilt
At my poor holding little would be spilt;
Small were the praise for singing o'er that wreck.
Who courts her dooms to strife his bended neck;
He grasps a blade, not always by the hilt.
Nathless she strikes at random, can be fell
With other than those votaries she deals
The black or brilliant from her thunder-rift.
I say but that this love of Earth reveals
A soul beside our own to quicken, quell,
Irradiate, and through ruinous floods uplift.

MY THEME (*continued*)

'T is true the wisdom that my mind exacts
Through contemplation from a heart unbent
By many tempests may be stained and rent:
The summer flies it mightily attracts.
Yet they seem choicer than your sons of facts,
Which scarce give breathing of the sty's content
For their diurnal carnal nourishment:
Which treat with Nature in official pacts.
The deader body Nature could proclaim.
Much life have neither.   Let the heavens of wrath
Rattle, then both scud scattering to froth.
But during calms the flies of idle aim
Less put the spirit out, less baffle thirst
For light than swinish grunters, blest or curst.

TIME AND SENTIMENT

I SEE a fair young couple in a wood,
And as they go, one bends to take a flower,
That so may be embalmed their happy hour,
And in another day, a kindred mood,
Haply together, or in solitude,
Recovered what the teeth of Time devour
The joy, the bloom, and the illusive power,
Wherewith by their young blood they are endued
To move all enviable, framed in May,
And of an aspect sisterly with Truth:
Yet seek they with Time's laughing things to wed:
Who will be prompted on some pallid day
To lift the hueless flower and show that dead,
Even such, and by this token, is their youth.

BRADBURY, AGNEW & CO. LD., PRINTERS, LONDON AND TONBRIDGE.